The Slow Turning Tide

Hastings in Austerity 1946 - 1954

Victoria Seymour

First published in 2008 By Victoria Seymour.

Email: mail@victoriaseymour.com

Website: www.victoriaseymour.com

ISBN 0-9543901-6-7

A catalogue record of this book is available from the British Library.

Printed in Great Britain by

impression IT
Unit 2, Maunsell Road
St Leonards-on-Sea,
East Sussex.
TN38 9NL
www.impressionit.co.uk

This book is dedicated to my son.

My special gratitude goes to the contributors to the chapters on "Post-war Citizens"

Hazel Comfort. Don Valentine. Ex-Inspector Charles Banks. Hilda Barker. Joan Henry. Joyce Brewer. Kathleen Upton. Marion and Arthur Henham. Moira Hornsey. Olive Peddlesden. Helen Bird. Pam Garnar. Phyllis and Ron Burkin. George Miller. Irene Burkin.

Thanks for help with research and for personal observations to Hastings and St Leonards History Consultants, Dennis Collins and Steve Peak. Fishermen's Museum Curator Phil Ormsby. Dudley Blois. Jean Gill. Nicholas Bacon. Pat Dunn. John White. Pat Connolly. Francis Cornwall. The Editor of the Hastings and St Leoanrds Obeserver, Peter Lindsey. Journalists Phil Elms and Ken McEwan. Hastings and St Leonards Observer Archive. Hastings Reference Library Staff.

Images provided by The Hastings and St Leonards Observer. Hastings Reference Library Collection. English Heritage. The Daily Sketch. Angie Quinnell. James Meredith. David Thornton. Ivor White. The Ken Brooks Collection. Pat Connolly Family Collection.

Services to the Author by Earlyworks Press.
www.earlyworkspress.co.uk

THE SLOW TURNING TIDE

1946

A German mine gently bumped its way shoreward between the piles of Hastings Pier. In the White Rock Pavilion opposite, the contestants in the first Annual Chess Congress since pre-war days remained oblivious to the looming danger. When informed of the imminent possibility of an explosion the organisers decided not to alert the contestants. The tense, final stages of several matches were in progress and they did not wish to disturb the atmosphere of concentration in the auditorium.

This was post-war Hastings, January 1946. After five years of enduring bombing, machine-gunning and random destruction by doodlebugs, a stray mine was a small matter to the town's people, particularly as it was the seventeenth to come ashore in the last week. The mine was carried eastwards where it was tossed about by the rising tide at Splash Point.

After lunch the families arriving to see the matinee of the pantomime "Mother Goose" at the White Rock Pavilion were shepherded by the police along the roads at the back of the theatre and down its side; on nearing the seafront entrance to the theatre, the adults and children were told by the police to make a run for it, in order to take their seats. Lieutenant Noel Cashford and the naval mine disposal party, based at Dover, were called. They arrived two hours later and the Lieutenant waded into the sea to recover the mine and after ten minutes expert work the detonator was removed. On 11th January three more mines were adrift off St Leonards; two became stranded on the beach by the western end of the promenade and the third continued floating by the wrecked St Leonards Pier.

Hastings and St Leonards had bigger things to contend with than the stray reminders of war washed in on the tide, chiefly its financial and structural recovery as a residential town and coastal resort. Even before the war ended Hastings began to look to its peace-time prospects: The business community realised that the quickest way for the town to recover was to exploit the assets it already had, its holiday accommodation and attractions. In an article published in a 1944 edition of the Draper's Record, Mr Clifford, Regional Chairman of the Defence Areas Hotel and Catering Industry Survival Movement wrote that the banned area seaside hotels would need vast supplies to make them ready to receive guests. For the affected towns he quoted figures in millions of the items needed; carpets, curtains, blankets, bed and table linen, towels and catering equipment. Added to this was the cost of repairs to the hotels and other accommodation that had been requisitioned for living and office space for the huge number of military personnel based in coastal towns, including Hastings. Hotels, large houses and all of the boarding schools had been requisitioned during the war and were in need of repair work and refurbishment. The shortage of residential housing was desperate. Bombs had destroyed or left uninhabitable 439 houses, and a further 14,818 properties were damaged. There was a proposed council plan to build social housing but these homes were designated for young families and there was a long waiting list, causing anger and frustration, as may be gathered from the following letter from a January 1946 edition of the local paper, The Hastings and St Leonards Observer. (Hereinafter called the Observer).

Dear Sir,
As I am number 1,400 in the local housing list may I ask if the council has any plan to erect prefabricated houses and if not why not? My husband, a RAF Flight Sergeant and Navigator and I have made fruitless efforts to get a home. We have been told we may eventually get a flat to rent for 35 to 40 shillings (£1.75-£2.00) per week. There is too much complacency on the part of those who already have houses.
Mrs Peggy M Wale, 187 Old London Road, Hastings.

Austerity restrictions on newsprint curbed Observer correspondents but the subject matter of their letters of 1946 have a contemporary ring – dogs fouling the pavement, the council's failure to empty dustbins, seagulls, either as nuisances or victims, children vandalising public gardens or breaking windows of unoccupied buildings. Topical arguments raged about the establishment of light industry on The Ridge. Others bemoaned the loss of Sunday milk deliveries and the behaviour of theatre patrons – arriving late or coughing and smoking during the performance. These letters were often drawn on for subject matter by the editor of the Observer, Frederick Goodsell, who wrote a column in the paper entitled “Flotsam and Jetsam” under the pen name “Vigilant.” This weekly feature gave him an opportunity to express his personal opinion on events in Hastings and the wider world. Goodsell was an old boy of Hastings Grammar School who joined the staff of the Observer in 1926 as a cub reporter. His abilities were recognised early, and on the retirement of the paper’s editor, Sir Alfred Dyer in 1940 Goodsell succeeded him aged only 31. In print he seemed very middle-aged by today’s perceptions; appearing by turns to resemble Victor Meldrew, Winston Churchill and Mr Pooter, but Frederick Goodsell’s attitudes are those of his period and station in life, and a guide to small town values. it is difficult to resist the temptation to poke gentle fun when in his column he tended to outrage or touched on lighter matters; if it is done here it is with affection.

The passage of time since Goodsell died makes it difficult to find people who really knew him. A local Evening Argus reporter, now in his nineties, recalls Goodsell as not a particularly happy man who lived with his mother, never married and did not seem to have close personal friends. The daughter of one of Goodsell’s contemporaries, an Observer reporter, said that her late father found his editor “heavy going” socially and that he seemed to be a “tortured soul.” Mary Barker worked at the Observer during and after Goodsell’s final years as editor. She has only a teenager’s recollection of Goodsell: “He was slightly built and reserved, a grey sort of man, lost in a big overcoat.” Current journalists have been able to provide further observations about Goodsell; Phil Elms, group production editor of today’s Observer had former colleagues who had worked with Goodsell in his later years. Phil gathered that the man was bad-tempered, opinionated and hands-on, adding, “He believed passionately in Hastings and ensured the Observer’s coverage was thorough and meaningful. You could read his paper years later and get a fair understanding of the town’s lifestyle. Goodsell was among the last of his breed.”

Ken McEwen, a journalist with almost 50 years experience, is the current Sports Editor of the Eastbourne Herald. He was interviewed in 1960, at the age of 15 by a frail looking Frederick Goodsell, for a job on the Hastings Observer. Ken felt that Goodsell had already made up his mind but he did him a favour by writing a letter to the editor of the Bexhill Observer, who gave Ken a job, leaving him thinking that the £10 he had spent on a new suit had not been wasted. After five years with the Bexhill Observer from 1966 Ken spent 13 years as sports editor on the Hastings Observer, by then John Cornelius had taken over as editor and Frederick Goodsell was consultant editor. Ken recounted that at one point the paper's owner, F J Parsons, suggested that Goodsell brighten up the Hastings Observer by putting pictures of pretty girls on its pages, to which he is said to have replied, "Fine but you will have to get yourself another editor." Ken said, "It was well known in his later years that Goodsell liked whisky, kept a bottle in his office and often seemed the worse for wear."

In the February of 1946 there were a number of complaints from West St Leonards residents that parts of their area were being used as dumping grounds for rubbish. Vigilant, having been on a weekend ramble, joined the complaint via Flotsam and Jetsam: *I was appalled to discover that tons of rusty barbed wire had been thrown over the East Hill Cliffs and left in a tangled heap near the refreshment hut. Gaunt metal structures and a brick wall, part of a former wartime training assault course still stand on the beauty spot. They should go as soon as possible - but not over the cliff!* He furiously reported a week later that assorted rubbish, including broken glass had been dumped on the beach near Rock-a-Nore, "spoiling a secluded cove and putting bathers in danger." At the news of Hastings Council workers being laid off and joining the ranks of the unemployed, Vigilant proposed that they could be re-employed painting and repairing the shabby and dilapidated public buildings such as the pier, or clearing rubbish, mentioning in passing the barbed wire below the East Hill Cliffs.

Austerity was biting hard; a world food-shortage had brought a return to almost wartime rations to Great Britain. The government announced that the wheat content of bread was to be reduced to wartime levels. Bread was not rationed during the war but from 1941, in order to reduce imports more of the grain was included in flour, producing a loaf which tended to look slightly grey. It was called the national loaf and disliked by most people. Butter, margarine and cooking fat rations were reduced in 1946 and there was no hope of an increase in meat, bacon, poultry or egg supplies. There was an urgent need to feed the 30,000,000 Germans who were threatened with famine as a result of the destruction of their agricultural industry. In an attempt to combat the widespread abuse of rationing in Great Britain there was a nationwide Ministry of Food campaign against food black marketeers. At road blocks vans and cars were searched for eggs, meat and poultry, which could bring more than double their fixed price when sold "under the counter." London market stalls were said to be running a flourishing trade in coupon-free clothing. The Observer reported hardly any accounts of Hastings black market trading convictions, but it may be that the years of rationing had sharpened the wits of such offenders. The nation was still being urged to grow and eat more of its own produce, to augment low rations and a poor diet.

Hastings received its first peacetime consignment of bananas on 1st February; they were destined for children and pregnant women only – holders of blue or green ration books. The bananas were stored to give them time to ripen and were ready for sale by Tuesday 5th February at 1/1d (5p) per pound. Teenager John White, who worked at Baker's the fish shop near a greengrocer in Robertson Street said, "People went mad when the first bananas arrived in Hastings after the war." A further delivery of bananas was promised in May, along with oranges, which were still only available to designated groups. Also in this shipment were onions from Egypt, but these were still in short supply and although not rationed they were to be shared out by allowing only 12 ounces per resident.

Hastings Council met in February to discuss a government report suggesting that in order to provide homes, existing properties should be converted. It was agreed that there were many such in Hastings that cried out for conversion into maisonettes of moderate size. "The chief obstacle, apart from materials and labour, is finance," said Mr A M Lupton, Chairman Executive of the Housing Centre. He requested that a government subsidy should be provided to aid the conversion work. Also discussed were the Marine Court Apartments; in spite of the numbers of military personnel decreasing by 60 to 70 per month the

ATS still occupied the building. The council was told, "There is no sign of the building being given over to its proper use and house agents say that they are getting constant enquires from prospective tenants for the 150 flats in Marine Court; the rent for the flats of varying size is from £85 to £400-£450 a month." Vigilant, quick to spot a contentious issue wrote: "Marine Court should be set free, its continued requisition is a scandal and the accommodation should be made available to the public without delay." Hastings builders Messrs Fryer and Sons said: "The construction and repair of houses is suffering delays of the highest degree, caused by Whitehall's form-filling demands and often the unavailability of the very forms required." Vigilant condemned the delays as, "A story of fantastic obstruction and government red tape at its very worst."

Government plans were underway to hold a military march and other events in London and nationwide to celebrate the two victories of 1945. On 9th March 1946 Vigilant wrote:

There is little enthusiasm for the victory celebrations in London. I have yet to hear a voice raised in favour of the parade that the government has fixed for 8th June. There are well-reasoned objections to a programme lacking in spontaneity and enthusiasm. The fruits of victory are proving bitter and peace difficult to establish and to make any elaborate show of rejoicing seems extremely ironical. We celebrated last year at the ending of the wars but have since entered a period of austerity at home and complexity abroad, which does not produce an atmosphere for whole-hearted public rejoicing. The nation is not in the mood for it under present circumstances. They have already had enough interruption to the tempo of life and the people should ask themselves that if they want both bread and circuses, where would these come from? Clothes rationing will prevent people from buying new attire for the occasion, the famine of cigarettes and alcohol and the lack of public transport will inhibit pleasure. There is a faulty psychology behind the victory parade.

The Hastings Member of Parliament, Mr Cooper-Key, who served in the Highland Light Infantry during the war, was against the parade and was among a group of MPs who tabled a motion in the House of Commons that the government should reconsider the matter. Hastings

1946

The St Leonards Bathing Pool

1946

Frederick Goodsell, Editor of the Hastings and St Leonards Observer
1940 to 1965

Lt Noel Cashford disables a mine on Hastings Beach

1946

The Hadley Page "Hastings" flies low over its namesake

1946

Entertainment Committee allocated £250 for local events to mark Victory Day.

Prefacing the first peace-time Easter holiday with an idea that was decades ahead of its time, Councillor E C V Symonds thought of new attractions for holidaymakers, proposing: "An ice rink scheme for the boating lake in the Old Town and Hastings Caves as a holiday show palace, with guides dressed as smugglers, figures of druids and prehistoric men and ghostly lighting." During the April Easter Holiday over 50,000 visitors flocked to Hastings but accommodation was 30% short. Visitors were told that they could demand three good meals a day on presenting their ration card but it was questionable if the ration allowance was enough for even two good meals per day and catering establishments were also sadly inadequate. A letter to the Observer suggested that if prefabricated houses were to be built in Hastings, when they had outlived their usefulness they could be adapted as surplus accommodation for holidaymakers.

The 8th June Victory Parade took place in London under grey skies and drizzle and the weather was no better in Hastings. There was church bell-ringing, a parade, mostly of sea and army cadets, a Red Cross contingent and an open air service of thanksgiving in Alexandra Park. There was a Punch and Judy show in Lower Warrior Square Gardens but it was Hastings Old Town that marked the event with style. The fishing boats were dressed overall, flags and buntings hung from buildings, a fancy dress competition, fireworks and a bonfire were organised. People stayed singing and dancing in the street until nearly midnight. Four of Hastings lifeboat men, Muggeridge, Adams, Martin and Edmunds marched in the London Victory Parade. Later relenting, Vigilant wrote. "While I remain out of sympathy with all the victory events, apart from the march in London, I admire the spirit behind them."

John Logie Baird died in Bexhill-on-Sea on June 14th, aged 58. The story was not front page news in the local paper. The significance of his invention had not yet been fully grasped. Baird had taken up residence in Hastings early in 1923, to convalesce from a bad bout of ill health. Over the following 18 months he carried out experiments that led, in 1925, to the transmission of the first true television image;

the painted wooden head of Stooky Bill at Baird's workshop in Frith Street, Soho. However it was in Hastings that he produced the first shadowy outline of an object, the shape of a Maltese Cross in his lodgings at Linton Crescent. Baird lived at 21 Linton Crescent for the duration of his stay in Hastings from February 1923 to November 1924. It was here that his first transmitting equipment was constructed. Following a demonstration to the press at Linton Crescent in January 1924 a report appeared in the Daily News. This information was passed on to Baird's father, the Rev. John Baird by a former congregation member. Baird sent his son £50, which enabled him to rent a separate workshop at 5 Queens Arcade. In 1997 a commemorative plaque was mounted at 21 Linton Crescent by the Institute of Physics.

In March Vigilant expressed his despair at the amount of bread that was being wasted locally. In April the Mayor of Hastings made a similar point to the Hastings Food Committee, saying that if every person in the country saved a matchbox sized piece of bread per day (holding a sample aloft) it would amount to 550 tons of bread saved daily nationwide. He was quoting from a letter he had received from the Prime Minister asking people to waste less food and grow more home produce. It was announced on the 29th June by the Minster of Food that bread rationing was to start on 21st July. Hastings bakers immediately expressed hostility to the scheme, pledging to fight for its abolition; one baker saying, "We bakers are given nothing but propaganda by the government, who expect us to make, and the public to eat, muck made with dud flour." The Hastings, Bexhill, Rye and District Master Bakers declared that the bread rationing scheme was unworkable and they would support their national association in fighting it.

The ration was set on a varying scale for different types of workers and children of different ages. For the ordinary adult the ration was nine ounces of bread per day, part of which could be taken in flour or cakes. The Food Minister's announcement was described by Winston Churchill as, "One of the gravest I have ever heard in time of peace." He demanded that figures of stocks and movements of cereals should be produced by the government to justify "this extreme measure." The Minister of Food, Mr. Strachey also announced that the meat ration would be increased by 2d per week from the same date.

1946

The bread and flour rations were allocated by coupons, or units as they were called, a system covering bread, flour, cakes, buns, scones and flour products not already encompassed by the points system. Allowances to catering establishments were restricted, but there were special provisions for industrial canteens and for the packed meals for workers on heavy manual jobs. Agricultural workers who were already getting the extra cheese ration were given additional bread units. The scheme introduced the most complicated rationing system which the British Government had ever imposed. The bread units for each week were the same figure as the daily ration in ounces. Thus the ordinary adult could have nine ounces of bread a day and the bread units per week were also nine, acquired by the use of coupons of varying values from the ordinary ration book. The decision to ration bread was an historic one for this country; it loomed during the later part of the war, especially when the German submarine attacks on merchant shipping were at their worst. It was ironic that in peacetime the populace had to accept this new food hardship. The purpose of the bread rationing scheme was to make British stocks and supplies last until the coming harvest, which promised to be good. The basic daily bread ration worked out at six average slices from the wartime loaf, which means the man in the street was expected to cut down his daily average of eight slices by two. Housewives thought that this new addition to the list of rationed food was the last straw. There were public protests by the Housewives League and in mid-July they presented copies of a 300,000 signature petition to the House of Commons and the Ministry of Food. Hastings, Bexhill, Rye and District Master Bakers suggested five ways to avoid bread rationing; registration of customers, the rationing of flour at source, separation of flour and confectionary (cakes) in the rationing scheme, the price of bread raised and no bread sold until it was 12 hours old. Other ideas were to institute a scheme as for milk rationing and not to have the bread units but a flat coupon rate for all, with one breadless day each week. Hastings housewives were not going to accept bread rationing without a fight, as letters to the Observer show:

Dear Sir,
I am enquiring if there is a local branch of the National Housewives League or similar in the town. I wish to organise a protest against the impending bread rationing. It would have the support of myself and

many housewives in the town.
Eva R McCoy of 6 Lower Broomgrove Road

Dear Sir,
I was asked by the Brighton branch of the Housewives League to start a branch in Hastings and I have already collected 450 signatures on a petition against bread rationing, which is to be sent to London this week. I shall be very pleased to hear from anyone who wishes to join us.
Mrs L Shrimpton, 28 St Mary's Terrace

A week after the start of bread rationing the Observer reported that on the first day of the scheme people had panicked and brought a tremendous amount of bread, redeeming more than their daily allowance of bread units. Cakes and buns remained unsold, resulting in waste of food. Alderman S Riddle of the Food Control Committee said that it would take time for the system to settle down. It appears from the following letter to the Observer that within a few weeks some people were coping quite well with the complexities of bread rationing, even though the local food office was not.

Dear Sir,
I have now cut my bread consumption by 50% so that I can get extra points for other foods in exchange for bread units, giving me a greater variety of diet, as promised by the Minister of Food. But when I applied to the food office I was informed that owing to the very heavy demand they were out of points. This is an important fact in the bread rationing scheme, suggesting that people are using less bread.
Mrs M Foster, 44 Marina. St Leonards

Vigilant said that the food office was under heavy strain and that he was pleased to note in the Hastings Municipal Journal an article headed "Hats Off to the food office." Bread rationing came to an end on 25th July 1948. It would be more correct to say that it just fizzled out as bakers had stopped bothering with taking bread units many weeks before the appointed date.

In advance of the 5th August Bank Holiday Hastings experienced the heaviest bookings for seven years. For this last public holiday of the year it was estimated that about 20,000 visitors would lodge in the town and about half of these would stay in private houses. The town was still 20% short of its pre-war holiday accommodation; the 1946 capacity of hotels and boarding houses was about 10,000. The crowds were expected to be swelled to 40,000 by day trippers. As it was there were 53,396 rail passengers and 9,000-10,000 arrived by car, making a total of approximately 64,000 visitors to Hastings, 25,000 of whom stayed over. It was believed that long stay visitors would spend £8 to £10 each per week and day trippers £1 each and that the total spent in the town would be not be less than £25,000. "Contrary to reports in the national Sunday press there were no people sleeping on the beach", said Hastings Borough Council. According to the Observer it was this weekend that B Riddle and G Veness started the famous Fish Museum on a barrow outside the fish market, displaying specimens caught in local waters and some rare catches, including an angel fish, a sting ray weighing half a hundredweight and a full grown barnacle found on the wreck of the Amsterdam off Bopeep. The star event of the weekend was the re-opening of the St Leonards Bathing Pool, which could accommodate 1,000 swimmers and 2,000 spectators. The new manager was Major Harold Pyecock, MBE, the former international swimmer and water polo player. The pool was commissioned by Hastings Council and built in 1932-33 at the cost of £60,000 under the auspices of Sidney Little, known locally as the Concrete King, the father of Hastings' 1930s concrete construction surge. Admitting 33,000 in June of its first year, the pool failed to make a profit thereafter and it closed it 1959. Under private ownership in 1960 the pool complex became Hastings Holiday Centre and included chalet hire for 300 guests. The pool and the holiday camp closed in 1986 and to date the site remains vacant.

The first Gala Night since before the war was held in Alexandra Park with the town band playing popular pieces. There was dancing on the lawn to the Demobs Dance Band, community singing with "Uncle Joe" and a performance by a trapeze act, "The Zeniths." Vigilant wrote of, "The Unrationed Joys of the Seaside… The crowds were controlled but contented, consoled for the lack of the little luxuries of pre-war summers by the unrationed joys of warm sunshine and by a sea that was at times like the proverbial sheet of glass." He followed this by a piece more in character; "Is your name on the elector's list to thus enable the authorities to serve the public more expeditiously?"

At Radlett in Hertfordshire on 7th September Hastings Mayor, in full civic state, gave the name "Hastings" to a new military transport aircraft designed and constructed by Hadley Page Ltd. An official statement prior to the launch described the choice of the aircraft's name as, "A suitable salute to this modern front-line town, whose roots are also deep in the historic past." Due to bad weather, flights of the "Hastings" were not possible after the naming but some days later it flew over the borough. Approaching from the west, the "Hadley Page Hastings" flew low along the seafront, banked and turned at Hastings cliff-top castle, circled over the town then flew back along the seafront at roof-top level, giving watchers an excellent view. The aircraft went on to assist in the Berlin airlift, and remained the RAF's main frontline transport aircraft for some 15 years, especially in the Middle and Far East. In 1950 Hastings Mayor presented Number 47 Squadron RAF Manston Transport Command with a plaque to commemorate the naming of the aircraft. The plaque was designed and executed by The Municipal School of Art; it showed the borough arms superimposed on a globe and surmounted by the winged badge of the RAF. When Britain withdrew troops from east of Suez the long range-transport had fewer uses. Many of them were put into store in the late 60s and broken up later, and many found their last resting place at RAF Shawbury. Some were later converted to weather reconnaissance as well as for training; the last of them were withdrawn in 1977.

In mid-September 1946 Hastings Town Council adopted a proposal that an application should be made for 500 pre-fabricated houses to be allocated to the borough, in order that some could be erected before April 1947; it would take six months to prepare the sites. Other steps were suggested to ameliorate the lack of housing; one being to extend the requisitioning of empty houses. Two weeks later the council were informed that 80 prefabs were on urgent order and this was the limit of the allocation to the borough. The prefabricated house sections were factory made, from wood and metal, some of which came from scrapped aircraft. The sections were delivered by road or rail and put together on a prepared base at the site. The services were then connected and the superstructure bolted together. This could take as little as three hours. The prefabs were a temporary solution to the housing shortage; they looked rather like American houses - a few were imported from the USA, but most were designed in Britain by the Ministry of Works. The amenities provided in the prefabs were ahead of their time and after early doubts occupants soon came to appreciate them. Most prefabs had 2 bedrooms, indoor lavatories, bathrooms, fitted kitchens with a fridge, cooker and solid fuel boilers that provided hot water. All this was luxurious to poorer working class people and a huge improvement in their quality of life.

The life-span of these temporary homes was reckoned to be about 15 years; they would probably have lasted much longer but the cast iron pipes that carried the services tended to disintegrate. Prefabs could be cold in winter, too hot in the summer and subject to leaks and condensation all year round. However, such was the popularity of prefabs that in parts of the country people queued all night at local council offices to be allocated one. Fights broke out in housing queues and new tenants were encouraged to make their new homes look occupied as soon as possible, to stop misunderstandings with desperate would-be prefab owners. The prefab estates tended to be full of young families, creating an instant community; some remember their lives there as one long party. Three-quarters of a million traditional brick homes were built by councils all over the country between 1945 and 1953. To make way for these homes the demolition of bomb-damaged homes and slums continued. In some cases good properties were knocked down, not because they were inadequate accommodation but to make way for big housing estates.

In 1957 local authorities were allowed to buy prefabs from the government for £150, as they were having difficulties building permanent housing quickly enough. Many prefabs outlasted their fifteen-year lifespan and local authorities faced resistance from their occupants when they wanted to knock them down. This is quite easy to understand, especially if the alternative was living in a tower block. Some people had in fact moved from larger houses to prefabs as they got older; rents were low and the homes easier to maintain and set in a park-like location with a good-sized garden. In 1946 some conventional building was underway in Hastings: On 10th October the first two brick houses to be completed since the start of WWII were occupied by Mr Kilbane and Mrs Shoesmith. The mayor handed over the keys to numbers 17 and 19, Old Church Road Hollington. As the ceremony ended the furniture vans drew up. The new houses were built by trade apprentices over a period of 12 months, on a site where two properties had been destroyed by flying bombs in 1944.

In late October a German V-antennae mine with an 80-day fuse was washed ashore by the Yelton Hotel on a Monday morning. Lt. Cashford said that more should be expected as there were still plenty in the sea. Another more welcome gift from the sea also arrived on Hastings beach: Wooden crates of tinned food, meat, jam and dried egg, cargo from a wreck on the Goodwin Sands. There was not a great quantity but the police warned scavengers that they risked having their bounty confiscated or being prosecuted if they helped themselves to the crates; they never-the-less did so.

There was good news on the housing front in mid-December: The 14-story Marine Court was sold and Mr West, of the agents Godfrey West and Hickman said that all the ATS would be gone soon after Christmas and the availability of Marine Court would do much to relieve the housing pressure on the town. This block of flats still stands today. It was built in 1937-38, after half of a Decimus Burton terrace was demolished to make way for it. The structure is in the style of an ocean-going liner and it was immediately at odds with the adjoining architecture. Time has done nothing to soften this stark contrast but along the way Marine Court has become a grade II listed building.

1947

The winter of 1947 was to go down in history as the snowiest since 1814 and among the coldest on record. The first night-frost came on the 20th January and winter began in earnest on the 23rd, when snow fell heavily over the south and south-west of England. The temperature seldom rose more than a degree or two above freezing and the snow built up. Across Britain, drifts more than five metres deep blocked roads and railways and many people were cut off for days. The armed services dropped supplies by helicopter to isolated farmsteads and villages and helped to clear roads and railways. Any breaks in the cold weather were short-lived. At the end of January snow storms struck Hastings, which was swept by north-easterly winds, creating blizzard conditions, the worst for years. Snow lay six to twelve inches deep and there were shoulder-high snowdrifts on the seaward-facing West Hill. The hilly nature of Hastings meant that public transport was often reduced or ceased because of the dangerous roads. Bus-user Vigilant commented grumpily:

Hastings residents have done more walking this winter since the bus strike in 1937 but one difference then was the readiness shown by motorists to offer lifts to those on their way to and from work. Today's drivers show a singular reluctance to help and many cars passed me by on my long trudge to the office. (It was indeed a trudge; Vigilant lived at 17, Glen Road, Hollington). One of the brighter features of the weather is the cheerful and active young men clearing house and shop fronts for a modest fee. These seem to be mostly workers who have been stood off due to the bad weather; they show a commendable enterprise and energy and use their time to the common good.

The unemployment figures at the time for Hastings and St Leonards were: Men 900, women 200 and juveniles 60. At least 50% of the male unemployed were from the building trade.

On Wednesday 29th January there were 21 degrees of frost and visibility in the channel was blotted out by whirling snow. In Hastings there were daily electricity failures at breakfast and lunch time. There was to be no let-up on the energy-saving drive, even in these bitterly cold weeks. The Hastings Town Crier was used to make public announcements about the fuel cuts, urging everybody to conserve yet more. The Hastings Gas Company asked the public to economise; local coal merchants would not deliver supplies to householders who already had a month's stock; cinemas opened later. Bakers said there would be a shortage of cakes but they would be able to supply full bread quotas. Street lighting was reduced and shops, offices and libraries were lit by candles, night lights and hurricane lamps. At meetings in the council chamber Hastings Town Councillors wore their overcoats under their robes of office and committee reports were read by the light of candles. These were also used to light cigarettes; the mayor was indulgent in the circumstances and smoking was permitted at an earlier stage of the meeting than usual. An air of mystery was given to a long corridor in the town hall by it being lit with just one candle at its end, "Acting as a beacon rather than as illumination," as the Observer's reporter wrote, commenting, "The old fashioned candle has assumed the importance of fully-fashioned nylons."

The February of 1947 was the coldest on record in many places. In some parts of the British Isles, snow fell on all but two days of the month; much of the snow was powdery and was soon whipped into deep drifts by strong winds. Householders were forbidden to use electricity at certain times of the day; teams of government inspectors were employed to seek out "pirates" using power illicitly. In an echo of wartime blackout regulations the aptly named Mr Frost, a seafront amusement caterer, who had left two landing lights on between 10.05pm and 1.25am in mid-February was given a magistrates' court fine of 10/- (50p) for wasting electricity. In early March the local paper reported amazing scenes, particularly on the Ridge, of everything being covered with glazed frost (frozen rain). The Ridge and the surrounding lanes were impassable by vehicles for three weeks. The branches of trees at the roadside and in the woods cracked and fell, with a sound like exploding bombs. Land girls were deployed to pull down the most dangerously hanging branches with ropes. Miss Emilie Crane, living at Lavender Cottage on the Ridge wrote to a relative in Canada:

1947

The sight of the frozen landscape was magnificent; like a pantomime fairyland. Telephone wires and tree branches were coated thickly with ice; folks came up from the town to just to see it. Sadly, birds died by the thousands and telephone poles crashed down into the road and hedges.

This spell was followed by gales and heavy snowstorms. Throughout the crisis, transport all over the country was seriously disrupted and emergency regulations added to the confusion. Food was in short supply and troops had to be called in to combat a further blow to the country, a road hauliers' strike. In London there were long queues at butchers' shops, some sold out. The fresh meat ration was reduced from 1/2d worth to 1/- per week, a cut in bread ration was predicted as wheat stocks were low. This led to a 50% reduction in beer production. Greengrocers limited customers to two pounds of potatoes each and other vegetables were in short supply. Economically, the country was almost on its knees. When the thaw came it brought a new disaster; after weeks of frost, the ground was frozen so hard the melt-water and heavy rain could not soak away. In East Anglia, where the major rivers flow north-eastwards, the south-westerly wind drove water before it; waves pounded the dyke walls and they gave way. Troops were called in, but they could do little to stop water pouring through the breached dykes and river levels rose, resulting in widespread floods. Thousands were made homeless and their possessions lost. Two million sheep were drowned and 500,000 acres of wheat ruined, which represented a month's bread supply for the nation. The misery of the floods continued into the spring. The situation was worsened by fuel and food shortages. Hastings residents, no stranger to flooding, even if it was of a far less disastrous nature, turned their thoughts to helping out:

Dear Sir,

As Hastings has escaped the floods it should adopt a stricken town or village and send the inhabitants part-worn but serviceable clothing and also money. The poorest parts of a town are nearest the river... Nobody has much to give away these days but many of us could add to the widow's mite.
Mr C. F Chinnery 131 Bohemia Road St Leonards
Vigilant drew his readers' attention to the paper's front page, where

1947

Hastings Mayor published an appeal for donations to the Lord Mayor's Distress Fund, set up to aid the flood victims.

In late March members of the Housing Committee and other officials made an evening tour of some of the proposed housing sites at Broomgrove, where it was planned to build 14 houses to replace the bombed steel homes. The new houses were to cost £1,350 each with a market value of £2,000. A visit was also made to the Seaside Road site at Marina, where nine prefabs had already been constructed, at a cost of £1,200 each. Three weeks later the Borough Engineer Sidney Little said that negotiations had been proceeding for some time for 34 houses to be built at Hollington; Messrs Jones Bros had been granted the contract and construction of the houses would cost £42,381.

In April Vigilant wrote of meeting with a former resident on an Easter visit to Hastings, who was dismayed to see:

The grim spectacle of Hastings Seafront and other prominent spots, where buildings stand empty, scarred and deplorably unkempt in appearance. When will the money and labour be available for this work and what of the bold schemes of the Borough Engineer Sidney Little? I am increasingly dubious about a policy which sterilises important parts of the borough and keeps them in shocking condition, while the fruition of ideals and schemes remain a matter for the distant future.

The Observer sometimes published the kind of story we have come to describe as… "And finally," for example:

On the morning of Saturday 10th May shoppers spotted a crocodile-like monster floating in the Bulverhythe Stream. Excited small boys threw stones at the mystery object and the bravest among them poked it with a stick, getting no response; some of the gathered crowd said it was just a log. Mr J Hope of 36 Bulverhythe Road finally captured the creature, which turned out to be a stuffed crocodile. He hung it on his clothes line to dry, hoping to use the skin but the long exposure to water caused it to disintegrate.

At the end of May, with a Bank holiday ahead the Divisional Food

Office advised that Whitsun visitors to Hastings should bring their own food. But the town's Food Control Committee felt that such advice was unfair to local shop keepers who depended on visitors as well as residents in order to prosper. A Food Executive said that there should be plenty of food in the shops over the holiday with the exception of bacon. The summer of 1947 saw the introduction of further austerity cuts as the nation's crises deepened; only miners, farmers and fishermen were allowed bigger rations of meat, cheese and eggs. The Whitsun weather was glorious and thousands visited Hastings. The pleasure ship "Glendower", which had served at the evacuation of Dunkirk, made its first sailing from the end of Hastings Pier since 1939; over 500 passengers took the round trip to the Royal Sovereign Lightship. Vigilant, in holiday mood, revealed an unexpected interest in male fashion:

During the last two weeks' heat wave men have found the clothing conventions weighing heavily. At the seaside there has always been a fair amount of licence in such matters but never-the-less older men can be seen grilling in lounge suits and waistcoats, with their only concession to the heat wave being an extra handkerchief with which to mop their brows. Younger men, probably ex-service types, wear khaki shorts and tunics and Burma Green sandals of eastern origin. Others think that a display of service-acquired tattoos plus slacks are suitable street wear, while the fair sex put to good sartorial use the ex-war department RAF escape maps that are printed on finest pure silk.

(Folded and tied, the maps served as fake blouse fronts or, more daringly, strapless brassieres, for swimming or sunbathing).

For men of Vigilant's generation having an undue interest in clothing was generally thought effeminate. Conversely, a young man's first suit was regarded as a rite of passage to manhood but too much looking in the mirror was definitely discouraged. For business and formal wear the suit still held sway, jackets were not removed in public places in even the hottest weather, as we have learned. Even while playing darts in the pub the working class man kept his jacket on. Not that he would have anything much in the way of special leisure wear. Casual clothes were often a previously good suit that had become outworn and had passed down a man's wardrobe hierarchy, ending its days as work gear.

1947

From the mid-1920s younger working class men began to affect the sports jacket and flannels outfit. These were usually worn with an open necked shirt, collar outside the jacket. This style created a clean, outdoor look and along with carefully combed and Brylcreemed hair it made a favourable impression on the girls. The more inhibited man added a tie to this outfit, just to show he had not completely forgotten how to dress correctly. Apart from soap, Brlycreem was probably the nearest most working class men came to toiletries; to use anything like aftershave or deodorant, even if they were available, was seen as unmanly; the view being that a man should smell like a man!

Sartorial conventions had changed during the war, when for men the finest outfit was considered to be a military uniform. On re-entering civilian life male service personnel were given a choice of suit and issued with a raincoat, a shirt with two detachable collars, a hat, a tie, shoes and two pairs of socks and two sets of underwear. Over two million "demob suits" were provided between 1945 and 1960. Two big north-east names in clothing manufacturing and retail, Jackson and Burton, supplied the demob suits but in only a few sizes, (the military uniforms they were replacing had been provided under the same "fitting" system). Each demobilisation clothing centre offered a slightly different suit and it was believed at the time that you could guess its origin from the style. Spivs, it was said, would hang round the clothing depots, offering to buy the ex-serviceman's box of new clothes. It has become a frequently-told tale that the box, handed over in exchange for five pounds, sometimes contained the discarded military uniform. This strikes me as highly unlikely; you don't get to be a spiv by taking things on trust! Further research revealed the truth about the fate of the discarded uniforms. Ron Burkin, who was demobbed from the RAF in 1948, said that he was instructed to keep his uniform in case he should be recalled to serve. He was also given a demob booklet, which he still owns, that includes rail travel and "sustenance" vouchers for the journey to a national emergency reporting point. His RAF overcoat ended its days being worn by his father as he drove a tractor over the wintry fields of a farm at Fairlight.

After the war women longed for feminine clothes that did not look like a civilian version of a military uniform, as did many wartime and post-war styles. A fashion revolution in the form of French designer Dior's

1947

Borough Engineer Sidney Little inspects Hastings first prefabricated house

The sea inundates Hastings Town Centre in a November high tide

1947

Icicles on burst pipes at the Observer building, photographed from a rear window of Hastings Library

The newly- refurbished Elite Cinema destroyed by fire

1947

"New Look" burst on the scene; it was a major turning point in women's fashion. In 1947 Christian Dior presented a style with a fitted jacket, a nipped in waist and full calf-length skirt. It was a dramatic change from wartime austerity styles. After the rationing of fabric and restrictions on design details during WWII, Dior's styles with their generous use of material were a delightful shock and Britain's fashion-starved women fell in love with them. Harold Wilson at the Board of Trade asked women to ignore the mode of longer skirts to save fabric, in the national interest. They didn't; one London store sold 700 new look suits in two weeks.

While Hastings was still struggling to recover a major disaster struck one of its entertainment venues. Just after mid-day on Monday 24th June and two hours before the re-opening of the newly refurbished and decorated Elite Cinema in Warrior Square, the building caught fire and quickly became a blazing inferno. Flames leapt 40 feet into the air and a great pall of smoke drifted over the town. Within half an hour two thirds of the cinema was wrecked and the remainder was badly damaged. The fire, of unknown origin, had started in the roof above the gallery; the blaze was fanned by a south-westerly breeze. With loud cracks, slates and splintered glass crashed into the streets below, where posters advertised next week's film; ironically "Blaze at Noon." Mr M Segal, Director of Hastings Entertainments Ltd and also of the De Luxe Cinema, had been testing the Elite's sound and lighting arrangements at mid-day and had gone out with Mrs Jay, another director's wife to buy some flowers for the foyer. When they returned about a half an hour later the building was in flames. The roof of the building collapsed at 12.30pm. There were no deaths in the fire but Fireman Cuthbert who had manned the lofty turntable ladder over the fire had both hands burnt, Fireman Scott of Battle was injured by a falling slate and Fireman V W Cole suffered injuries from falling debris. The damage to the cinema was estimated at £100,000. Four days later Vigilant expressed in his weekly column his sadness at the loss of the Elite and wrote something of its history.

The theatre opened on 13th October 1879 under the name of the Warrior Square Opera House. When the Prince and Princess of Wales came to Hastings to declare open Alexandra Park on June 26th 1882 they lunched with 400 guests in the reception room of the opera house.

1947

The building was the leading centre of local entertainment and social functions; the young Winston Churchill lectured there on his experiences in South Africa. World famous opera singers performed in the theatre, later renamed the Royal Concert Hall. By contrast it was also used as a roller skating rink, with patrons circling on wooden-wheeled skates, "making a roar like Niagara Falls", as one person observed. The theatre became the Elite Picture House not long after the end of World War One. The Elite was damaged by bomb blast in 1940; the commissionaire was blown through the doors but was only slightly injured. In 1942 St Columba's Church opposite was demolished by bombing, causing serious damage to the Elite, which was thereafter used as a store by the Admiralty.

The ruins of the burned-out Elite Cinema stood for a number of years until they were cleared to make way for a block of flats.

On 17th July floods caused havoc in Hastings Town Centre after a four-hour overnight storm in which two inches of rain fell, causing hundreds of pounds worth of damage. Water welled up through drains bringing with it evil-smelling rubbish and black mud. The water swept in a torrent through Middle Street, Station Road and Priory Street. A commercial artist had his whole business wrecked: On his demob from the RAF he had set up a flourishing sign-writer's workshop in middle Street; as the waters subsided he found everything in the shop coated in black mud. The boiler room in the town hall was flooded to a depth of four feet and the inner yard of the police station, adjoining the town hall, was also under water. The town centre cricket ground became the usual after-flood boating lake. The event made national news and the WVS in Tunbridge Wells sent Hastings a van filled with mops, buckets and cleaning materials as well as items of household linen. Hastings' Mayor set up a disaster fund for local flood victims, which by the end of August had reached £425.Vigilant commented that the problem in Hastings Town Centre flooding called not for palliatives but radical treatment to affect a permanent cure. In late July Hastings Borough Council held its longest debate for years on the subject of the flooding; the Borough Engineer Sidney Little said that no ordinary system could have coped with the volume of rain that fell on the night of the flood. A Fairlight reader of the Observer proposed to the council a cure for the flooding problem that surely met Vigilant's description of "radical"; in short, it was that the Ore Valley should be dammed. The picture in this book of Hastings Town Centre inundated by the sea has proved impossible to date. The flags around the Albert Memorial signify an occasion of celebration and the still semi-screened shop fronts, a wartime blackout and bomb blast precaution, suggest it is a period not long after the war. The photo may have been taken in November 1947, around the time of the royal wedding. So commonplace was the phenomenon of town centre flooding that the law offices in Middle Street would expect to be flooded about four times a year, coinciding with high tides and always in the first week of August. The water welled up through the office floorboards and was not considered to present any real problem unless it reached the knees of the staff. A stock of Wellington boots was part of the office equipment and the lower drawers of filing cabinets were never used, as a precaution. At some time a faucet had been installed in the office to wash away the post-flood residue which was partly sewage sludge. References tell that 1949 was the last time the sea flooded the town centre.

Floods of another kind were dominating the local news, as the paper predicted "Holiday Tide at High Level", referring to the amount of visitors expected in Hastings for the August Bank Holiday. It was widely publicised that due to improved accommodation there was room for all comers and a big holiday amusement programme was ready. With his eye for detail Vigilant was at his most Pooterish, grumbling about the out-of-date entertainment posters to be seen about the town:

I include those for the White Rock show "Twinkle" and Ivy Benson's Dance Band, long since over. I have often noticed the apparently imperishable nature of advertising placards in our public places. They should be removed, as allowing them to remain courts dissatisfaction and inconveniences visitors, who are misled by information that no longer applies.

Hastings was accustomed to visits from famous people from the worlds of the arts, politics commerce and entertainment but considerable excitement attended the arrival in Hastings of an outside broadcast unit and the BBC celebrity, Richard Dimbleby. (As a war correspondent he flew in a RAF Lancaster bomber on raids and was the first journalist to witness and describe the horrors of Belsen). Richard Dimbleby came to dominate post-war radio and later, television, commentating at the funerals of King George VI and Winston Churchill, and the coronation. Dimbleby's purpose in Hastings was to record an episode of "Down Your Way", an immensely popular Sunday evening Light Programme feature. Each week residents in different towns were interviewed, each concluding with a piece of music of the subject's choice. Mr Dimbleby was guided round the Old Town by Police Sergeant Tester, making cheery encounters with Hastingers, including John Burton, who was Hastings Pier Master and Mr W Ashdown, a car park attendant. The last call was at the Prince Albert Public House, to meet the Winkle Club Secretary Bunk Harffey. Bunk was installed in an upper room of the pub where the club used to meet; much jollity ensued in the finding of a microphone lead long enough to go up the stairs.

By early October 30 aluminium temporary bungalows (prefabs) were being erected at the rate of one an hour in Coventry Road, Hollington. However progress at the Rock Lane new houses building site was not all it could be, due to a shortage of labour. During the summer the work had also been delayed by a union dispute. By late September the foundations only had been laid for 40 to 50 houses and 20 houses roofed in. As a stop-gap many local families had been found homes in requisitioned buildings. There were 1,864 families on the Hastings and St Leonards' housing waiting list.

In mid-October came a story that sounds like something out of the television archaeological series "Time Team." There were revelations of a secret wartime installation at Beauport Park Hotel: The Observer reported:

Experts, along with a German four-man prisoner of war working party were sent to Beauport Park grounds on the Ridge to investigate a subsidence. Shallow excavations uncovered oak planks that were concealing an entrance to a series of amazing tunnels and chambers, constructed by Canadian soldiers in the middle of the war. Should Britain have been invaded by the Germans in WWII the bunker would have been a hiding place for bands of highly trained and daring men who would have fought behind enemy lines. It is understood that similar underground chambers have been discovered in other coastal areas.

Bonfire Night celebrations were the biggest the town had seen since 1938; bonfire societies long since dead were revived. A procession wound through the main streets of the town, revellers carrying 150 coloured hurricane lamps. There were bands, decorated floats and children pushed Guys in prams. There was a fancy dress competition; a huge bonfire on the beach at Rock-a-Nore; the burning of a 17-foot Guy on the West Hill and fireworks from the cliffs. Vigilant saw it as, "The popular revival of old time pageantry."

Pageantry on a regal scale was to follow: In a speech Sir Winston Churchill described the wedding of Princess Elizabeth and Prince Philip on 20th November 1947 as, "A flash of colour on the hard road we travel", which sounds like mere rhetoric until the event is viewed in its setting. The nation was weary of austerity and the wedding spectacle was indeed a flash of colour; eager spectators had slept on London's pavements overnight, reserving the best spots from which to see the wedding procession. This was the first time I and others had seen a royal occasion on television; my family was invited into the house of my parents' employers to watch events on their set.

Princess Elizabeth's dress was designed by Norman Hartnell. It took a team of women seven weeks to create the dress from panels of pure silk, ivory duchesse satin, heavily embroidered with seed pearls, crystal beads and silver thread; the dress cost £1,200; a huge sum in 1947. To placate a rationing-afflicted public the palace announced that extra clothing coupons had been allocated and that some of the lace had been supplied by the bride's grandmother, Queen Mary. A few members of the Labour Government of the day were hostile to what they saw as inappropriate displays of extravagance in a period of severe austerity. Others objected to the use of pure silk for the dress, believing the fabric to be the product of former enemy countries - Italy or Japan. In fact the fabric was made in Scotland from thread produced by the silkworm farm at Lullingstone Castle. The dress had a 13 foot (4 metres) train of ivory silk tulle edged with satin flowers and was made in Braintree Essex. The Princess carried a bouquet of white orchids which after the ceremony were placed on the Tomb of the Unknown Warrior in Westminster Abbey. The chief bridesmaid was Princess Margaret, who like the five others, wore a dress of white tulle and duchesse satin. The two kneelers used during the service were covered in rose pink silk. When they were reupholstered for the service to mark the couple's diamond wedding anniversary it was discovered that the wood bases were made from orange boxes, date-stamped 1946.

With rationing still in force the reception was an austerity affair for 150 guests. It was a simple menu by today's standards; sole, braised partridge with green beans, potatoes and salad followed by ice-cream. Apart from a wedding toast from the King there were no speeches. Lady Pamela Hicks, one of the bridesmaids, recalled sixty years later that the youngest bridesmaid, Princess Alexandra, aged 12, ran around boisterously at the reception; Lady Pamela said, "There is always a young bridesmaid wrecking the reception, isn't there?" She also said that as chief bridesmaid, Princess Margaret bossed the others around. Queen Juliana of the Netherlands noted how dirty everyone's jewellery was. Prince Philip was upset that his three German sisters were not invited. Lady Pamela said, "I think Philip understood, but the sisters certainly didn't. For years afterwards, they'd say, 'Why weren't we allowed to come to your wedding? We weren't exactly storm troopers.'"

The royal couple were given more than 2,500 gifts from all over the world; all were listed in an official wedding present catalogue, regardless of their value or who sent them. A dinner service from the French government and a piece of cloth woven by Ghandi were named alongside homely gifts from the British public; a handmade afternoon tea cloth, a pair of nylon stockings, a silk-covered hot water bottle and two hand-knitted cot covers. There were also consignments of food from the Empire such as 500 cans of pineapple, a commodity practically unobtainable at the time. The food was made up into parcels by teams of Women's Voluntary Service workers and distributed to the needy. On the 14thApril 1948 Mrs F W Sinden, aged 84, of 131 Parker Road Hastings became one of the lucky recipients. Enclosed was a letter from Princess Elizabeth saying that the contents were sent from overseas as royal wedding gifts and hoping they would be accepted with her very best wishes. Mrs Sinden's daughter, Mrs F M Taylor said that her mother was very pleased with the parcel.

In spite of the national mood of celebration, austerity attitudes were still very much in evidence in Hastings when the Chief Constable, Lt Colonel A G Cargill, refused a licence extension for the Royal Victoria Hotel dinner dance, to celebrate the royal wedding. He said: "Those who wish to pay their respects to the royal couple can quite easily drink their health before 10pm!" The royal wedding did bring a temporary lift to the dreariness of austerity and flags fluttered from Hastings Albert Memorial, hotels and public buildings. Shops put on red, white and blue window displays and Plummer Roddis and Mastins featured bridal gowns in their windows. The Ritz and Regal Cinemas opened during the morning to allow the public to enter free of charge and listen to a broadcast of the marriage ceremony; there were large audiences. Restaurants served what they called wedding lunches and they put slices of wedding cake on the afternoon tea-tables. Where did they get the ingredients?

As Christmas approached, Hastings butchers were told by the Ministry of Food that there would be no pork for the ration. The hotels in the town were surprisingly well booked for the holiday, even though some hoteliers feared that the low level of basic petrol ration would keep visitors away. In December 1947 a 600lb food consignment, sent from Canada to the people of Hastings, was packed into 74 individual parcels and distributed to local ex-serviceman and the elderly. Vigilant made what was for him an annual appeal. "You are aware from these columns of my support of the Christian Alliance of Women and Girls providing a happy time at Christmas to young women who would otherwise be lonely. The war disrupted the CAWG plan for a holiday home for its members. Now a large, well appointed house has been secured at 62 London Road for this purpose and the alliance is appealing for cash donations from the public." After a Christmas Day of high winds and rain, Boxing Day brought brilliant sunshine and cloudless blue skies; people were strolling along the seafront or sitting in the promenade shelters. It was concluded that in spite of austerity most people had had a good time. Vigilant wrote that there was no rationing of fun and kindness; then he reminded readers:

1947

If a cut in the size of newspapers is to be avoided in the coming year, it is imperative that a greater proportion of waste paper must be made available for the production of newsprint. Paper salvage is still as important to the nation as it ever was. I hope that local salvage efforts will be intensified. Every household and business can help by saving every scrap of paper for collection.

The Hastings and St Leonards Observer was still under austerity newsprint restrictions, having only ten pages. Consequently, coverage of events tended to be selective, concise or held over for several weeks; press photographs and adverts were also very limited.

1948

Hastings greeted the New Year, according to the Observer, "With public scenes of revellry, after a year of national crisis, relieved only by a golden summer and the happy pageantry of the royal wedding." The "revellry" was put into perspective by the report that about one hundred people were at the Albert Memorial (Hastings Town Centre), defying heavy rain to see a performance, given on a temporary stage by the pupils of the Phyllis Godfrey Dance School.

The first four Rock Lane houses were completed and the new tenants, chosen under the town hall housing points system, were scheduled to move in on Monday 12th January. The houses had three bedrooms, modern kitchen fittings, bathrooms, coal sheds and perambulator stores. In Hollington several houses were roofed in and almost ready for occupation. All of the borough's supply of prefabricated homes were completed and occupied. With regard to more permanent homes, Councillor S W Thorpe said that the government would not allow any new contracts for building but that existing ones could be completed. Following the publication of this news there was a flurry of irate letters to the editor of the Hastings and St Leonards Observer, one from an ex-serviceman who was angry to learn that one of the Rock Lane houses went to a couple with one child, while he, his wife and three children struggled on in temporary accommodation.

Vigilant, returning to his wartime Churchillian style renewed the call for the town to save energy:

Economise on the use of electricity between the hours of 7.00am and 7.00pm. We are all in this together and should never forget that our own lapse into wastefulness may impose acute discomfort on the whole community. Employers and Trade Unions throughout the South East are urging that Fuel Economy Committees intensify their efforts in the next few weeks.

There was very little industry in Hastings in 1948 but that which there was organised night shifts to spread the load; it was fortunate that it was a mild winter.

Borough Engineer Little introduced his newest town plan on 17th February, at a meeting held to look into the town council's application to compulsorily purchase more than 60 bomb sites in Hastings. Little's scheme was to construct an underground civic conference hall beneath the White Rock Gardens, connected to a hotel on the seafront by an underground passage. One of his other ideas was that traffic should travel part of London Road St Leonards on an elevated road with the shops beneath. The local paper devoted almost its whole front page to Little's plans, including a design of his subterranean conference hall; generous coverage in the time of a newsprint shortage.

A correspondent with an idea before its time wrote to the Observer at the end of February:

Dear Sir,
With reference to pensioners and buses: Some time ago I visited a town where old age pensioners were given free passes to be used only during certain hours of the day, excluding of course the times needed for workers. There are many old age pensioners in Hastings who would greatly appreciate this concession, leaving room on the buses for the busy folk when they most need it.
Mr E W Loader. Major, Salvation Army,

The publishing of this letter prompted Vigilant to give forth on one of his favourite subjects; the local public transport system. It happened that the Maidstone and District Motor Services, along with the other companies that operated the Hastings area bus services were embarking on a campaign to encourage reciprocal courtesy between passengers and staff. Vigilant wrote;

The campaign idea has been given the blessing of the Hastings Mayor, Councillor F W Chambers but local residents want a little more than courtesy from its public transport operators, for example; better services in various parts of the town, especially the Hollington route. Due to timetable changes passengers have been receiving anything but courtesy in certain instances and much misunderstanding could be avoided by explaining properly these changes to staff and public.

In March the government announced a cut in the cheese ration from two ounces to one and a half ounces per week per person. Things were much worse for the population of Europe, as can be learned from a letter in the local paper that begged for money,

To buy relief supplies from Australia in the form of shark liver oil, lard, dried and skimmed milk, herrings in brine and orange juice, for the children and elderly in the refugee and displaced persons camps in Europe.

As there was a ban on leisure motoring people mostly travelled to Hastings for the April Easter by train or coach. In spite of this, hotels and boarding houses had plenty of bookings and the town saw 40,000 visitors. A holiday attraction was the bullet-proof Mercedes Benz of German Field Marshall Goering, visiting Hastings on its nationwide exhibition tour, raising funds for British military charities. The notorious vehicle was on show for one week at Skinners Garage, 18 Cambridge Road. The car was discovered by British forces in Germany, Lentenford, Schleswig-Holstein. It had five-ply, one and three-quarter inch thick glass bullet proof windows and specially fitted steel sides and floor to give protection from grenades and mines. The car had been lavishly equipped but most of its accessories had been removed by souvenir hunters. Based on a model on sale in England in August 1939, the adapted vehicle weighed over five tons and had an 8-cylinder supercharged engine with 7.7 litre capacity. The public paid sixpence each (approx 3p) to view the car and to receive a souvenir pamphlet. The director of Skinners, Mr Michael Hickman, drove Goering's car along the seafront to Wellington Square where he was joined by Hastings Chief Constable Lt Colonel A G Gargill. After Mr Hickman drove the Mercedes to the Bathing Pool, Cargill took over the wheel and drove it back to the town. They stopped at the Gaiety Cinema in Queen's Road where a large crowd gathered to examine bullet marks made by the British Army during tests on the car's windows.

Sixty years later the Observer was instrumental in helping to find local people who had seen Goering's car: Mr Nicholas Bacon still has the leaflet from the exhibition. He said, "I regarded the car as just a battered machine from the war and at the time it didn't move me at all." Pat Dunn, who was a student at the time, said that she volunteered to the sell sixpenny tickets at Skinners, "People were very interested to see the car in which Goering had stood, giving the Hitler salute." Pat was studying at the Hastings School of Art, regarded as rather prestigious at the time. She said: "A lot of mature students went there; men who had come out of the forces and wanted to advance their careers." She remembers the now famous artist Arthur Johnson as being one of these and Ted Drury, who went on to draw cartoons in the Daily Mirror. Pat said,

Growing up in Hastings after the war was an exciting time as far as I was concerned; there were youth clubs, our evenings spent playing table tennis and netball and there were sports organisations, including cycle speedway – remember the Rock-a-Nore Rockets? Then suddenly you were old enough to go dancing on Saturday night and out came the taffeta dresses. Admission to the pier ballroom was two shillings (10p); if you were flush, for half a crown (approx 13p) you could go to the White Rock lower hall, dancing to the "Harmony Aces". Your parents were catered for too; there was the Chamber of Commerce Ball, long frocks for ladies and dinner jackets for men and the overpowering smell of mothballs! Summer Sunday nights were great, with many of the famous big bands and artists; Ted Heath, Joe Loss, George Shearing and Hoagie Carmichael, being led on stage by Stefan Grapelli. The White Rock Pavilion was always packed for the summer shows; Clarkson Rose's Twinkle and the Fol de Rols. It was time of processions; the town carnival, Youth Week, Guy Fawkes – any excuse. There were gala nights at the bathing pool, dancing and firework displays at Alexandra Park. After the dreariness of war Hastings became alive.

In April, the Fuel Minister, Hugh Gaitskill, said that motorists would be rationed to 90 miles per month from June. This was causing local and national concern among those in the holiday trade and a group of all-party MPs pleaded for petrol concessions to help the plight of seaside and holiday towns. As if to compensate, 12 extra clothing coupons per person were to be made available from May until the end of September. A further sign of the easing of austerity was the government announcement that the end of rationing of footwear and furnishing fabrics would come into force by 9th September.

The controversy that surrounded the setting up of the National Health Scheme (later called Service) was becoming evident nationally and locally. Medical consultants and specialists in the London area voted by 766 to 11 to reject service under the National Health Act 1946. One hundred and one of the doctors of Hastings and St Leonards attended a meeting at the Castle Hotel in Wellington Square to vote on the National Health Act in its present form; 94 voted against, six abstained and one was in favour. Doctors feared becoming paid servants, without a say, in an administration run by civil servants, even though Aneurin Bevan offered doctors freedom of partnership and practice under the NHS. In mid-April a meeting to discuss what would happen when the state took over the hospitals was held in Hastings; it was believed at the time to be the first meeting of its kind in the country. The Hastings Area Hospital Management Committee was addressed by Mr Julian, Chairman of the South East Regional Hospital Board, who was accompanied by other board officials. Mr Julian, in answering criticisms that the National Health Service would be impersonal, said that the notion was rubbish: "We shall increase the amount of sympathy shown to the patients and their relatives."

It was very hot in May 1948; the water in the St Leonards open-air bathing pool was 67 degrees. Fridges in businesses all over the town broke down, unable to cope with the extreme temperatures; it was 89 in the shade. Hastings Chief Constable warned residents and visitors of the dangers of too much sunshine. The same month saw an unappetizing report from the Observer:

The Hastings Food Control Committee has mentioned complaints that corned mutton sent from Australia tastes of iodine. Although the Sanitary Inspector has described the meat as unpalatable due to excess preservative the public are none-the-less requested to eat it, to help out the butchers.

In June Hastings Round Table distributed 700 food parcels from Canada at the Old Town Hall in the High Street. Stored in the building's basement were further consignments of food from Australia, Hastings New Zealand and other towns and it was thought that, "Altogether, the Dominions have been most helpful."

On 12th June Vigilant lit upon a subject which was worthy of his ability to express righteous indignation; it was the film "No Orchids for Miss Blandish", which was to be screened in Hastings. It was a British made gangster movie that starred only one US actor, the rest of the cast being British, assuming very bad American accents. The film's content was very violent and sexual for its time and it attracted hostility from many quarters, including Vigilant:

I am glad to see that the Rural Dean, Rev J C Poole has challenged the Hastings Watch Committee's decision to allow the showing of "No Orchids for Miss Blandish", provided that the cuts made to the film's showing in Hastings are the same as those made at the request of the London County Council. Eastbourne has banned the film outright, as should Hastings, especially during this, Hastings Youth Week, the object of which is assisting the town's young people to grow up to be clean, decent and law-abiding citizens.

The public outcry from some quarters at the film led Harold Wilson to say at an industry banquet, to loud applause, that he was glad there were no Oscars for Miss Blandish. The film was shown in Hastings at the De Luxe Cinema from 28th June, returning in July for further week's showing, "By popular demand."

The Borough Publicity Officer and Rotarian W H Dyer was reported as having made a valuable contribution to the town when speaking to a local club on the subject of "Talking Up Hastings," a catch phrase which I had believed to be a late 20th century notion. Dyer suggested that residents should praise the town in their letters to family and friends because, "Too few people in other parts of the country realise what Hastings has to offer." A visible aspect of austerity in the town seemed to be receding; brighter street lighting was to be permitted but the Electricity and Public Lighting Committee said that restrictions would not allow ornamental lights on the promenade bandstand. In the same edition of the Observer Vigilant wrote a paragraph on the seafront floral display, saying, "It is lacking and compares badly with

1948

Hastings Chief of Police drives Herman Goering's car along Hastings Seafront

A section of Mulberry Harbour washed up by storms on St Leonards Beach

1948

Sidney Little's revolutionary plan for Hastings Town Centre

An Observer photographer with a sense of humour records autumn floods

Eastbourne and Bexhill. There is nothing to charm the eye and all seems bare and dreary."

The headline on Saturday 3rd July Observer, two days before the NHS began was, "Hastings Prepares for new Health Scheme" continuing:

Over 48,000 citizens have enrolled before the appointed day and 6,000 medical cards have been issued. Up to 1st July 1948 51 doctors in the borough have applied to enter the scheme; one of them for maternity cases only. It is expected that all of the chemists and opticians will take part. In the short time since the invitation to dentists were issued only so far five have decided to join the NHS. Patients are free to choose the doctor they want or to continue with their present doctor. Hospital charges will cease on Monday.

With continuing food rationing, a housing shortage, spiraling tuberculosis death rates and following the exceptionally severe winter of 1947, the inception of a welfare state could not have come at a better time for post-war Britain. We take the NHS for granted now, but before 1948 proper health care was something that not everyone could afford. There was a strong feeling that the British people should be rewarded for their sacrifices in WWII so in 1942 the government asked Liberal Party member, Sir William Beveridge, to write a report on the best ways of helping people on low incomes. In December 1942 Beveridge published his report, which proposed that all people of working age should pay a weekly contribution; in return, benefits would be paid to people who were sick, unemployed, retired or widowed. Beveridge believed that this system would provide a minimum standard of living, "Below which no one should be allowed to fall". These measures were eventually introduced by the Labour Government that was elected in 1945. In the following year the new Labour Government began the process of implementing Beveridge's proposals, the basis of the modern welfare state. The driving force behind the NHS was the charismatic Minister of Heath, Aneurin Bevan.

The arrival of the NHS made a difference to everybody's life although not everything changed immediately; no new doctors were appointed and no new hospitals were built. What had changed was that poor people had access to proper medical services. Previously, many often went without medical treatment, turning instead to questionable and sometimes dangerous home remedies or to seeking the charity of those doctors who gave their services free to their poorest patients. A visit to a doctor was free to workers on low pay but this didn't cover their wives or children, nor did it cover workers with a better standard of living. Something like a quarter of hospital beds were provided under voluntary schemes. This facility varied from those in small hospitals in lesser towns, supported by public subscription, to internationally famous teaching hospitals such as St Bartholomew's, Guy's and St Thomas's. Special hospitals concentrated on particular diseases or types of patients, children or women. The remaining hospital beds were provided by the local authorities of counties and large towns. These provided municipal hospitals; maternity hospitals, hospitals for infectious diseases like smallpox and tuberculosis, as well as hospitals for the elderly, mentally ill and mentally handicapped. The standard varied widely, depending upon the attitude of the council. Mentally ill and mentally handicapped people were generally locked away in large forbidding institutions, not always for their own benefit but more to save other people from embarrassment. Older people who were no longer able to look after themselves also fared badly. Many ended their lives in the workhouse, a Victorian institution feared by everyone, where paupers did unpaid work in return for food and shelter. Workhouses changed their names to Public Assistance Institutions in 1929, but their character, and the stigma attached to them, remained. The NHS took control of 480,000 hospital beds in England and Wales. An estimated 125,000 nurses and 5,000 consultants were available to care for hospital patients. A total of 2,751 hospitals came under the control of regional health boards. By 10th July 1948 over 53,000 Hastings residents had joined the NHS and 56 doctors were taking part. Nearly all the town's opticians had joined, as had all chemists. The participating dentists had increased from five to twelve. It was estimated in 1948 there was a shortage of 48,000 nurses but by 1952 the situation improved; figures show there were 245,000 whole time equivalent nurses.

One of the early tasks of the Hastings Group Hospital Management Committee, which held jurisdiction over the area's 14 hospitals, was to decide upon a new name for the Municipal Hospital - Hastings Union Infirmary or the "Muni", as it was called by locals. The original use of the building was as a workhouse, accommodating the poverty-stricken able-bodied who could work, the sick among them who could not and itinerants, (tramps). From 27th August 1948 the institution officially became St Helen's Hospital, adopting the name of the parish in which it stood. Medical Officer Doctor Leonard Booth saw the hospital through its period of change, becoming under the NHS the Medical Superintendent of St Helen's Hospital. The first Secretary of the new group was Mr H A Froggatt and the administrative offices were in Holmesdale Gardens, Hastings, behind the Royal East Sussex Hospital. The new regime brought about the immediate cessation of casual accommodation for tramps at the Municipal Hospital and the progressive transfer of able-bodied elderly inmates to local care homes. By the spring of 1952 the hospital group comprised entirely of NHS beds; twelve of which could be used by private (fee-paying) patients.

The introduction of the NHS encouraged thousands of sufferers from chronic, minor and major ailments, who had thought it was their lot to endure until incapacity or death intervened, to seek medical help. Those in need of treatment for poor eyesight, bad teeth and varicose veins thronged surgeries and the NHS resources were being used up very quickly. From its earliest days, the NHS seemed to be short of money. Annual sums put aside for treatments such as dental surgery and glasses were quickly exhausted. The £2 million designated to pay for free spectacles over the first nine months of the NHS went in six weeks. The government had estimated that the NHS would cost £140 million a year by 1950. In fact, by 1950 it was costing £358 million. However, the popularity of the NHS meant that in the 1950 election, the Conservatives promised to keep it; Labour won the election and in 1951 introduced a charge for some dental treatment and for prescriptions for medicine. Aneurin Bevan resigned from the government in protest at this. He wanted a free health service and would accept nothing less.

On July 24th the Observer said that St Helen's Hospital was short of maternity rooms and the management committee called for an immediate inquiry into the situation as a matter of urgency. Doctor Booth sent a letter to the committee saying that the accommodation had been overloaded for some time. Maternity wards and home midwives all over the country were busy; figures showed that the birth rate was the highest in the UK for 26 years. This was ascribed to couples 'catching up' on the lost the war years and decreased infant mortality. Princess Elizabeth joined the baby-boom when it was announced that she was expecting a baby in the autumn. In October there was a hint of local disenchantment with the NHS when the Observer headlined, "Is This the Cinderella of the Town's Hospitals?" St Helen's Hospital was experiencing staffing difficulties and the Hospital Group Management Committee considered the vexed question of the admission of chronic sick to St Helens, stating:

In the past all municipal hospitals, as was St Helens before 5th July, were obliged to accept such cases. But the former municipals are adopting the same procedure as other hospitals and the responsibility must be accepted by the service as a whole. The prevailing situation is making it difficult to recruit nurses as they do not like caring exclusively for the chronically sick. If nothing changes at St Helen's Hospital the stigma of it once having been the workhouse infirmary is going to continue to be attached to it. A special place should be provided for the old.

At the start of the summer's factory and school holidays Vigilant offered some advice on how to get the best out of a holiday. It was his opinion that it should be divided into thirds; one for rest, one for recreation and the remainder for worship. He also devoted a paragraph to "The Danger of the Handkerchief":

For mopping-up operations of a personal kind the handkerchief has a practical purpose in both hot and cold weather, far outstripping its decorative value. But scientists tell us that these useful objects convey germs in their thousands, which can be passed on by handshakes and in the confines of a crowded bus. We shall do well to use our handkerchiefs with more care in the knowledge of the possibility of the dangers of spreading infections.

A danger of a more explosive kind than sneezes was brought to the attention of Hastings Police when they received an urgent telephone call from the Royal Engineers, stationed in a unit in North Sussex. An R. E. officer explained that for some time he had been engaged in checking that all the anti-invasion demolition explosives had been cleared away from various locations in the area. He had discovered that the high explosive charges buried under the foundations of the Harrow Bridge had never been cleared. A section of Sedlescombe Road North and the Ridge highway were immediately closed and the occupiers of properties near the bridge were kept at a safe distance, while the explosives were safely removed.

The animosity to modern town planning continued in Hastings. In a talk to the Hastings and St Leonards Museum Association in November Mr Anthony Dale, the Brighton author, made a plea to Hastings Council to preserve buildings of historic and cultural interest. Mr Dale sharply criticized the deplorable attitude of councils in coastal towns to their heritage buildings. "From Lyme Regis to Margate councils have destructive records equal to none." He said he believed that the Regency period was the last great era of English architecture, referring to the work of Decimus Burton in St Leonards.

Public rejoicing broke out in Hastings on the night of Sunday 14th November when it was known that a son had been born to Princess Elizabeth. Most people heard it on BBC radio at 10.20pm but the news soon spread throughout the town by word of mouth. The bells of Blackland's Church rang out only a few minutes after the official announcement. Next day many other churches rang bells, the Union Jack flew from the town hall and all public buildings and people put flags in their windows. The Mayor sent a congratulatory telegram to the new royal parents from the people of Hastings. Five children were born at St Helen's Hospital on the 14th November, three girls and two boys. The boys were Anthony John Chinnock and Alan John Smith.

It was announced in December that the Old Town Hall in the High Street was preparing to assume its new role as a branch library and museum in February 1949; the building continues as a museum to the present time. Rector Rev. Leslie Hook said that the Fishermen's Church at Rock-a-Nore would not be re-opening; it had been closed during the war and used as a military store. The pews, pulpit, choir stalls and other church furnishings would be sold and the church pulled down under a corporation planning scheme for that part of the town. The rector said that only £15 compensation had been paid by the War Office and it would need £150 to the make the church fit for use again.

Built in 1854, it was described as a Chapel of Ease. Happily it escaped the town planners and in 1957 it became the Fishermen's Museum but is still used for religious ceremonies – the annual harvest festival, carol concert, baptisms – nine or ten in 2007 and for memorial services.

American students from Hastings on Hudson sent 6,000 bars of milk chocolate to Hastings England to be distributed to the town's school children – one for each child. The town got ready for a bumper Christmas as far as visitors were concerned. Out of the 93 large residential guest establishments only one intended to close for the holiday and the town's 539 boarding houses expected to do good business. After expressing routine seasons' greetings to his readers, Vigilant had a grumble about the mean thief who stole a Christmas cake from a colleague, when he left it in his car, parked outside the Observer Offices in Cambridge Road. As a bit of Christmas cheer Vigilant announced that the government limitation on circulation figures was to be lifted early in 1949 and there would be more copies of the Observer.

1949

The town was shocked to learn of the sudden death from a heart attack on 15th January of Hastings Mayor Alderman Chambers, a Freemason, who was in his third term of office; he had been ill for only a few days. The event dominated the week's news. A civic funeral was held at St Clements Church; the list of mourners was of such length that it spilled over from the front page of the Hastings and St Leonards Observer into three further columns inside. On the funeral route the traffic was controlled for the first time in Hastings by police use of "walkie-talkie" equipment. Three weeks later Hastings had its first woman mayor in the 360 years since it had received its charter. The new mayor, Mrs A W Farnfield, agreed to hold the office until the completion of the municipal year. She was to be addressed as Madam Mayor; Alderman H Burden was deputy mayor.

A previously anonymous Hastings benefactor was revealed with another death in early January, of a man who had been a "Father Christmas" to the poor families of Ore Village. The secret philanthropist was the late Mr W H Langdon, a solicitor of the Hastings firm Young, Coles and Langdon. For 25 years Mr Langdon had sent anonymous gifts of coal, meat, fruit, vegetables and groceries to these families, who never knew who was the donor. Mr Langdon's agent in the good deeds was the local Public Health Department Welfare Officer, the appropriately named Mr A E Christmas, whose work brought cases of need to Langdon's attention. The provision of the gifts had continued throughout the war, with rabbit being substituted for lack of meat supplies. Family butchers were still having a testing time in 1949. At a meeting of the Hastings and St Leonards District Meat Traders Association, the Hon Sec, Councillor A J Oliver, said that in every other trade things were looking up but all the butchers could look forward to was maintaining the 1/- per week meat ration. There was a general dissatisfaction with the quotas of offal; one butcher complained that he had been given only two ox livers to share between 500 customers. One trader said it was heartbreaking to be a butcher these days and he longed for Saturday nights, so that he could shut up shop and forget it all for a few hours. Bacon was also a problem for suppliers; the ration was two rashers per person per week; sometimes there was not enough to supply all the shops. A grocer, Mr C R Clements of 84 Milward Road, displayed his bacon slicing machine in the shop window, dressed in mourning drapes and funereal flowers and bearing a sign, RIP.

An exhibition was held at the White Rock Pavilion in February to display the council's "New Look" for the town. One of the models was of the proposed marine viaduct and sea lagoon between Rock-a-Nore and Ecclesbourne Glen. Part of the plan was that the cliff-face should be floodlit at night and speed boats would operate in the lagoon by day. On a newly extended Old Town Promenade there would be a miniature railway, a car park at Rock-A-Nore and a tea chalet at Ecclesbourne Glen. The biggest plan was for double-decker road at Hastings Town Centre, giving the pedestrians traffic-free access to the shops below. Along with this went a plan for an underground bus station in the below-promenade car park. To complete the scheme a road was to be excavated under the houses at the top of Wellington Square, to connect with the road behind. Vigilant asked:

Is this the Hastings we want? I went to inspect the scheme that Sidney Little's bold and imaginative mind has evolved. Many visitors to the exhibition thought that the plan should have been far less ambitious. The thousands of pounds it requires to construct gave the whole thing an air of unreality. Quite a few expressed, in an ironic sense, the opinion that it would be many years before Hastings could find the money for these spectacular projects; one saying he hoped it would be 40 years on. But first the Hastings eyesore bombed sites must be dealt with before the holiday season starts.

A month after Little's exhibition Vigilant was demanding, "Hands off Old Town", warning that priceless features of the Old Town might be swept away, once the Hastings Corporation development schemes began to take place. He said that it would be a tragedy for Hastings to lose its precious heritage and it should not be allowed to happen. At a council meeting Councillor Major Sims-Hilditch raised the point that £20,000 per year in rates was being lost due to unoccupied bombed sites. An enterprising individual displayed a second hand car for sale on the large bombed site in Havelock Road, where the buildings on either side of the empty plot were shored up with crude, gallows-like timber supports. An Observer reader came up with a camouflage idea:

Dear Sir,
...On the matter of the ugly bombed sites in Hastings: I suggest that wooden screens could be erected to hide the grisly background on Hastings Seafront.
These screens could be bordered with a neat moulding and painted with colourful marine or pastoral scenes by theatrical scene painters or pupils at the local School of Art. These would surely stand for a year of two...
Mr C F Faulkner of 16a Chapel Park Road

The writer continued by making unfavourable comparisons between Hastings and Brighton's better efforts in dealing with this problem, by shielding bombed sites from the eyes of passers by with rows of large, potted trees. This moved Vigilant to comment that Brighton probably had more money than Hastings to do this sort of thing but it showed a spirit of progress and anti-defeatism. Hastings was a relatively poor town, post-war. The police still administered the charitable fund established in 1914 with a legacy from a Mr Alfred Pett of Hastings who left £500 to Hastings Corporation to be invested and the interest therefrom to be used for the sole benefit of the deserving poor children of the town. Mr Pett directed that the money was to be used for buying clothing, boots and food, whenever necessary. The will also laid down that the fund was to be administered by the Chief of Police of Hastings and his force, adding the hope that others would contribute to the fund. Hastings Police continued this beneficent work throughout WWII. Vouchers were issued to hard up families and a supply of clothing was kept at the police station for needy cases. The fund operated up until the 1960s.

Under a headline on 26th February "Frightening Cost of National Health Plan", the Observer article quoted from a talk given to the Robertson Street Senior Men's Forum by Doctor T Parkman, the Deputy Medial Officer of Health. He said:

The ultimate cost of the NHS, as assessed by an expert could be in the neighbourhood of £500 million per year. The public must be sensible, or the scheme will fall to pieces or at the least go bust in parts. In the first six months of the new medical service people made such a rush at doctors that patients were not getting the same attention as previously. Doctors are being shockingly overworked and underpaid.

In June a dentist wrote to the Observer about complaints that dental patients were unable to get emergency treatment. The unnamed dentist said:

As far as dentistry is concerned the NHS should have been introduced gradually; children first and then mothers and so on. As it is I am working beyond my limit, making new sets of dentures for the elderly, who under previous circumstances would have made do quite well with what they already have. I regard the dentist's main job as being relieving pain and preserving teeth.

On March 15th clothes rationing ended; this had been in force since 1941. The utility scheme, in which garments were made under a cloth quota system, continued and clothing price controls stayed. Vigilant advised residents to put their unused clothing coupons in the salvage collection. "If all the 48 million clothing coupon books are salvaged it would amount to 670 tons of waste. Nearly 1,400 tons of waste paper are needed every year to make spools for the cotton spinning industry." Sweet Rationing ended at midnight on 23rd April; it had been in force since July 1942. Mr Percy Idle, Chairman of the Hastings Food Control Committee said that no new confectionary shops were to be licensed "Small shops selling sweets have endured a very lean time and now that rationing has ended they ought to get some benefit." Sugar for domestic use remained rationed. The confectionary industry was allowed only 54% of the sugar it had used pre-war but it gave a warm welcome to the news of the end of sweet rationing. A spokesman for the Cocoa, Chocolate and Confectionery Alliance stated that they were very glad about the de-rationing and they would do everything possible to make it work. During the war the price of sweets and confectionary had doubled; many people had not been using their ration coupons, which had been increased to 6 ounces per person per week by 1949. The nation immediately went mad on buying confectionary and within days sweet shop shelves were bare; this shortage stirred up Observer correspondents:

Dear Sir
Is there no way of stopping people in the town buying so many sweets? Now there is a shortage. I overheard a lady, who was standing in front of an empty sweet shop window with a friend say that she had been all over Hastings and St Leonards that morning and succeeded in buying 30 pounds of sweets. It is time the attention of the Minister of Food was called to his de-rationing of sweets.
St Leonards Resident.

The writer must have felt vindicated when it was announced that sweet rationing was to be re-instated. Many said that the April confectionary buying panic was an example of what would happen if food rationing was ended.

Mayor Mrs A W Farnfield opened the 1000th council house constructed in Hastings and St Leonards under various housing acts since 1920; the house was 43 Mountbatten Close on the Rock Lane Estate. No tenant had been allocated to the property. The list of corporation accommodation provided since the end of the war was: Permanent houses 125, prefabricated houses 80 and units under requisition 341 – a total of 546 homes. A further 80 houses were under construction and were being handed over at the rate of two per week. Tenders for 278 houses and flats had been accepted; the work was already started and was to be completed in 12 months. Hastings Corporation released these figure to scotch rumours that only 100 homes had been provided since 1945. Hastings held its first town carnival since pre-war days. Hastings Seafront was lit up again, from the Carlisle Hotel to Marine Court, at an installation cost of between £600 and £700, costing 5/- (25p) per hour for current; the lights would be switched off at 11pm. The carnival queen for Hastings' first carnival since the war ended was Jean Horsfall. She was crowned by stage and radio star Betty Astell. She was accompanied by her husband, comedian Cyril Fletcher, whose first stage appearance had been at the White Rock Pavilion in 1936, in Newman's "Fol de Rols". The carnival week was one of brilliant sunshine and packed with events to please the holiday visitors. The purpose of carnival week then as now, was to raise money for local charities. The 1949 event produced a profit of £2,281, £1000 of which went immediately to the Old People's Welfare Fund, the selected beneficiary of that year's carnival. The week was marred on 28th June by an accident to the 20-foot high chair-o-plane ride at the carnival fair on the Oval. The ride collapsed with all of its chairs occupied. A bystander said that the top of the attraction seemed to slip sideways, slow down slightly then fall with a loud crash. Several people were trapped beneath the wreckage and others crawled out with assistance. There were no severe injuries but 24 people were slightly hurt. The most seriously affected was June West, aged 17, who suffered a cracked bone in her right arm.

In early July Hastings doctors reviewed the first year of the NHS; a well-known local doctor, who would not be named, gave his views on the operation of the service with special reference to local problems. He referred to an "absurd" statement by Mr Aneurin Bevan to the effect that there were an adequate number of doctors in Hastings; in fact it was over-doctored. The doctor said. "The ratio only applied to the population figure as a whole and did not take into account the fact that Hastings had the highest average age of any town in Great Britain. Additionally, as a health resort it attracts more sick people. It would therefore be obvious to anyone of even the meanest intelligence that more doctors would be required here." The anonymous doctor was correct in saying that Hastings had a larger proportion of old folk than anywhere else in the country. Many of these could not make ends meet, although 40% were eligible for some kind of non-contributory pension, which they had never claimed. The Honorary Secretary of the Hastings Optical Committee, Mr E G L Thorpe, wrote to the Observer explaining that the delay in patients receiving their new spectacles would be between six and eight months and the situation was worsening. Demands were greater than the industry could supply. Three million pairs of spectacles were uncompleted, the chief difficulty being in supplying lenses. The official figure for the total cost of the National Health Scheme for the Hastings area in its first year was £206,955. In July 1949 the government announced that the NHS was costing more than had been expected; 2/6d (Approx 13p) per week per head, 1/4d (7p) more than first calculated. At least some attempt was being made at savings – The Royal East Sussex Hospital in Hastings published a letter of thanks in the Observer to those townspeople who had kindly supplied old stockings for use in the plaster bandaging department.

A mass observation survey on the NHS, conducted in 1949, brought predictably varied responses:

The service is getting abused. People are using any old excuse to go to the doctor when they would not have previously troubled him.

The doctor does not seem as friendly as he used to be. He just a civil servant and doesn't want to do any more than he has to.

I think that the National Health Service is good on the whole but people abuse it.

There are extravagances on the part of doctors. It's a waste of money; I'm sure the poor could be helped without it.

I don't feel we have a family doctor any more and the surgeries are crowded.

Some felt it had created a beneficial medical equality, others that it encouraged malingering. Many believed it had introduced regimentation to medical care.

Vigilant welcomed the re-introduction of sweet rationing on Sunday 14th August:

It will deprive residents of the sight of holiday-makers spending the precious hours of their visit to Hastings in waiting for the erratic opening of seafront confectionary shops. To see day-trippers wasting two hours of their six in the town in queuing, within view of the delights of the beach and sea convinces me that people enjoy queuing. They are a nuisance on the front, taking our police away from more important duties to supervise the throngs that block the entrances and window displays of neighbouring businesses. Our own well-mannered residents have scarcely tasted a sweet all summer but after tomorrow there may be a few lollipops left for local children.

A keen theatre-goer Vigilant complained that the White Rock Pavilion had to be put to so many other uses. "Mr Kenneth Day, Director of Entertainments could have secured a week's engagement of the operetta “The Chocolate Soldier” but the hall was required for the yearly garden produce exhibition. Until the town has another civic hall for conferences and big meetings the pavilion will never settle down as an entertainments centre. It will be a happy day when it ceases to be an all-purpose parish hall.” He was no doubt pleased when the gardeners were told later that it was their last time at the White Rock Pavilion as their reservation was to be taken over by a show called “Evening Stars.”

The Hastings and St Leonards Television Viewers Club was believed to be the largest outside London. The club made two visits to Alexandra Palace where they were present during a transmission from the studio. It seems that one of the main reasons for local viewers forming a group was to investigate cases of interference with TV reception. In September they were pleased to say that in most cases it was possible to detect the source of the trouble and stop it, when neighbours understood how their apparatus interfered with reception.

In September the milk ration was cut twice, from three pints per person per week to two and a half; a week later it was cut yet again to two pints per week. In October the price of petrol was increased by two and a half pence to 2/3 (12p) per gallon. A recipe section in the Observer explained how to extend the meagre ration of bacon by using it as part of the filling for jacket potatoes, suggesting; “You could add an egg if you can get one”.

On 3rd October it was announced in the Observer that the Borough Engineer, Mr Sidney Little planned to retire in February 1950. He was described in the announcement as:

The man who made modern Hastings and an expert in concrete construction and although some of his schemes came in for criticism no doubt he showed great foresight in all he carried out.

Late October brought the wettest week since meteorological records began in 1875; there were torrential rain squalls and wind that reached 60 miles an hour; tremendous seas flooded the town centre; emergency supplies of food were organised by the School Meals Sub-committee and delivered to flood-trapped families. The heavy seas re-floated a 30 foot section of a Mulberry Harbour, which had been resting at Bulverhythe since the previous November and cast it up again on the beach opposite to Warrior Square, from where it went out to sea then drifted landwards, putting the safety of Hastings Pier at risk; it finally ran aground further along the shore and was dismantled.

In early December, 20 German children from Berlin, ten boys and ten girls, aged between nine and fourteen, arrived in Hastings for a three month stay. They were just some of the 400 German children brought to England in 1949 under a special scheme. The children were welcomed at the Trades and Labour Club in Robertson Street by their foster families, in a parody of the British wartime evacuee scheme of ten years previously. The children had been travelling for three days without a break; the last part of their journey involved a three-hour ferry crossing from Ostend to Dover in a gale and a two hour coach trip to Hastings, during which the children sang German folk songs. The children looked pale and tired; they had all lost their fathers in the war and were being brought up by mothers who had to work. It was hoped that the children would gain weight and improve in health during their visit. The foster families had already filled Christmas stockings and parcelled up gifts for the children and invitations to at least six parties were awaiting them.

1950

To give more coverage to the forthcoming General Election in February 1950 the size of the Observer was temporarily increased to 10 pages; newsprint was still severely rationed. Restrictions were reinstated in the following autumn, with a return to austerity-sized newspapers. Hastings anticipated a three cornered fight; the candidates were: Cooper-Key, Conservative, Cohen, Labour and Hurd, Liberal; at that time Hastings was a traditionally Conservative constituency. Campaigning was vigorous and feelings ran high, indicated from Vigilant's 4th February piece:

"When Parties go Astray." It takes a General Election to transform certain normally sensible people into fantasy-mongers, with more guile in them than one would believe possible. Last week's leading article in the Observer appealed for restraint and truth in local electioneering but I fear it is too much to hope that this appeal will be met with an all round response. I publicly deplored the action of the Holy Trinity Ward Conservatives in throwing away the opportunity to have Mr R F Boutwood as their chairman and therefore it is assumed I am a Tory. May I respectfully remind the imaginative people who, disliking a piece of honest criticism, take refuge in spreading baseless rumours. My party allegiance is my own affair and no business of theirs. It is the policy of the Observer to give a fair show to all the parties.

An election rally was held on 18th January at the White Rock Pavilion, where the three candidates spoke and answered questions. Huge interest was shown by local voters. The theatre was filled to its 1,200 capacity, with the audience already seated half an hour before proceedings began. Queues for admission had formed three hours ahead of the start of the rally and police turned away hundreds who could not get in. There was a good voter turnout on 23rd February; patients from the Royal East Sussex Hospital made their way to polling stations on crutches and in one old folk's home 86% of the residents voted. The town's leading confectioner, Henry King and

Fiest, played it safe with a celebratory cake for each party displayed in their shop window. There were 70 polling stations in the constituency; ballot boxes from the rural areas were delivered to Hastings by lorry with a police escort. The count took place in Hastings Pier Pavilion with 70 people counting votes and 10 or 12 supervising; the result was expected by 2am. Predictably, the Conservative candidate, Cooper Key, won with 30,035 votes and increased his majority from 3,597 to 12,432. Labour polled 17,603 and Liberal 9,122. Nationally, the Labour Party was returned to government with a majority of only six.

As the election results were being counted a desperate search was taking place on the isolated Fairlight cliff area; two boys from the Doctor Barnado home in Old Roar Road had disappeared in a minefield at Fairlight Glen. The boys had been out walking with two others who had returned home safely after dark but Roy Rutherford, 12 and Keith Hamfrey, 9 lingered behind. The boys became trapped 80 feet up a cliff and 20 feet inside an uncleared minefield. The police, coastguards and members of the life-saving auxiliaries searched in pitch blackness, fog and rain; the boys were found and rescued at 4am. Instrumental in the rescue, while risking their own lives, were Coastguard Station Officer A G Dickenson, Coastguard J Paine, along with Mr F Cruttenden and Mr E Brazier. After their rescue the boys were rushed to the Royal East Sussex Hospital where it was said they were comfortable but suffering from raised temperatures. The danger of the beauty spot was highlighted the following week in a letter to the Observer from Major W E Carter of Boma Cottage, Fairlight. He said that it was extraordinary that nothing had been done to clear the mines before life was lost and that surely five years after the war Hastings Borough Council should have made this area safe. Hastings Town Clerk replied say that the area was fenced off and signs saying "Danger Minefield" had been erected. Adding that due to the configuration of the terrain and the risk of landslides it was impossible to do anything for the time being.

The Hastings Television Club, which by now had 100 members, travelled round the district tracking TV interference sources in a private car equipped with direction-finding apparatus. When discovered, the owner of the offending electrical item was asked to have suppressors fitted to it. If this was likely to cause financial hardship the TV club paid. An example of this was the case of a local taxi firm whose cars were fitted with suppressors at the club's expense. Production of TV sets in Britain suddenly increased in 1950 by 250% but this was not reflected in television ownership in Hastings.

For many years the Observer ran a children's section for the Little League of Kindness, otherwise known as Uncle Jim's Corner. Apart from publishing jolly little pieces, Uncle Jim encouraged children to help good causes by collecting farthings, silver paper and used postage stamps. It was a front page news item when the LLK was able, with added contributions from several businesses and government offices, to donate £120 to various local good causes. Uncle Jim wrote that he was very proud of his nieces and nephews. In fact "Uncle" was none other than Vigilant! One might think that this role did not sit well with a crusty bachelor but it is said that he would often delegate the column to one of the women on the paper's staff.

In early March the council proposed more ambitious plans for modernising Hastings and the memorial changes were approved. A bus station on the seafront at Caroline Place and the exclusion of public service vehicles from two main shopping streets were proposed. Perhaps of more immediate importance were the plans to re-build on the bombed sites at White Rock, Warrior Square, and Grand Parade, St Leonards. Included was a long-term plan to complete the promenade in front of the Royal Victoria Hotel and the widening of London Road by stages.

The German children who had been staying in Hastings since December 1949 left the town in March, looking much fitter than when they had arrived thirteen weeks previously. The children had attended twelve parties, visited London and had been pupils at local schools during their visit. They departed clutching bags of oranges and apples. Food rationing in Germany ended on January 16th 1950; in Britain the Ministry of Food continued to publish regular bulletins in the national and local press informing people of the fluctuating values of the points in their ration books. No wonder people used to say that Britain won the war but lost the peace. During the war and the austerity period, the Borough of Hastings was estimated to have received a quarter of a million pounds weight of foodstuffs in bulk supply and individual parcels from the Commonwealth and America. Hastings was invited to contribute to the Lord Mayor of London's National Thanksgiving Fund Appeal, launched in gratitude for the generosity of friends and kinfolk overseas. Vigilant endorsed the appeal and asked locals to give generously. In August Vigilant returned to the subject of the Lord Mayor's Thanksgiving Fund:

The total value of food sent to Britain by America and the Commonwealth during the war is £80 million. The total value of the subscriptions to the Hastings contribution to the thanksgiving fund is £287, which even in hard times can scarcely be regarded as creditable for a town of Hastings' size. Let us not say that we failed to show gratitude for the benefits we received. The money raised will chiefly be used to provide a home-from-home in London for men and women students from overseas, giving us the opportunity to create friends for Britain for generations to come.

By September Vigilant reported that the Hastings donation was still under £300 and suggested that if everyone who had received a parcel subscribed only sixpence or a shilling the sum would be greater. He wrote:

Latest figures revealed that the Lord Mayor has so far received nearly £68,000, mainly from businesses and industry and in addition to the money raised by local committees, leaving over £1 million to be found as Britain's thank you.

By October there was news of setting up a Hastings committee to add to the £298 collected to date; November found this figure unchanged and Vigilant pressed his readers to make it £650. One may wonder why Hastings, which raised millions of pounds during the wartime fundraising weeks devoted to special causes were so reluctant to give. Possibly the purpose of the fund was the stumbling block; asking a population suffering from a crippling housing shortage to help buy a home for students on an overseas "holiday" seems not well devised.

The abolishing of the points system for certain foods at the end of May brought no rush to the shops at Hastings. The scheme had been in force for eight years, as a wartime measure but it passed away peacefully.

One trader said that business had been pretty brisk with sales of plain and fancy biscuits, jellies and treacle but he thought that housewives were being governed by their pockets. Canned and dried fruits were also off points but in such short supply that allocations were already exhausted before the points scheme ended. There was a run on syrup, as sugar was still rationed. The following week, removal of petrol rationing on May 16th brought a pre-war level of cars to Hastings at Whitsun; they were parked in line along the seafront and all the car parks were full. Deputy Chief Constable G Sheppard said that the standard of driving was not all that it could be; people were in too much of a hurry but the incident and accident rate was low. Motorists celebrated by burning books of petrol coupons and a garage owner papered a petrol pump with discarded coupons. The price of petrol increased again, bringing to it just under three shillings (15p).

In July Hastings Borough Council approved the sum of £10,000 for expenditure on celebrating the Festival of Britain. The sum was to cover illuminations; four fountains on the seafront, further floodlighting of Hastings Castle and transferable lighting that could be used on the seafront or Alexandra Park, with the cost of these attractions to come out of the rates. The Entertainments Committee turned down the suggestion by the East Sussex Publicity Club that the 1066 invasion should be re-enacted as part of the Festival of Britain celebrations. Councillor Rymill supported something more permanent, rather than a pageant that would be forgotten in three months. Vigilant challenged:

"Is this the best use of £10,000? I imagine the ratepayers will be about as enthusiastic at spending this sum on illuminations for Hastings to mark the Festival of Britain as the general public is on the festival project as a whole. Residents would prefer the money to be spent on overhauling Hastings amenities or disguising the bomb sites, improvements to the covered promenade (Bottle Alley) and remedial treatment to the seafront flower beds, too shallow and exposed to be attractive. To many minds the idea of lavish outlay on the Festival of Britain grows increasingly unpalatable as national commitments to anything but the festive increase. Municipal economy is preached but sometimes none too widely practised and it is difficult to feel happy about the council's decision.

1950

For Vigilant the Festival of Britain was the Victory Parade of 1946 all over again. Local residents were as hostile to the spending as Vigilant, as the Observer letters column reflected:

Dear Sir,
The figure of £10,000 to be spent on entirely unproductive displays seems to me to be quite iniquitous. As a ratepayer I protest most emphatically at such an appalling use of public money especially when economy is so essential.
Rose Matthews, 3 Blomfield Road, St Leonards.

Dear Sir
...This is a wicked waste of money and of no value to the town. If the council must spend another £10,000 there are many things of much greater urgency than having the town lit up more than it already is."
John E Ray. 9 Stanley Road Hastings.

Another correspondent's outrage led to unintentional humour:

Dear Sir
The £10,000 should be used to help the sick and the old. Spending on public lighting will only encourage the ice cream cornet-licking, rock-sucking type of trippers, who lounge about our streets, displaying a parade of more tongues than in a doctor's surgery. The better taste of our resident population should be considered.
Name and address supplied

On Sunday 10th August the town's war graves were hallowed at an open air service in Hastings Cemetery. The Observer reported:

Although marred by brief but heavy showers it was a memorable and impressive occasion. There was a large gathering to witness the dedication of the graves of servicemen and women and civilians who died between the years 1939 and 1945 as a result of enemy action. A number of the military personnel and the 134 listed are buried elsewhere in the cemetery.

The plot for the war dead is known as Heroes Corner. The Rev A E

Gould, President of the Hastings Free Church Council officiating at the service declared, “The victims died for beliefs that the world still needs.” Harry Henham, aged 19 was the first soldier to be laid to rest in the Heroes’ Corner; he is mentioned twice in my previous books. In 2008 I received a touching letter from his younger brother, Arthur, who had just discovered Harry’s name my first book. From Arthur I learned more of his brother’s short life. He said.

He was six-foot tall and a great swimmer, he would dive off the end of the Harbour Arm and swim to shore. He loved dancing - I used to meet him from work with his going out clothes so he could go straight to Hastings Pier Ballroom. Harry joined the army and in May 1940 he was waiting on the beaches at Dunkirk, already wounded and was picked up by one of the Armada of little ships that went to the rescue of the stranded army. He was in a boat when they were machine-gunned by a German plane and Harry sustained a head injury. He survived until he arrived at Brighton hospital but died there. My dad went to pick up his body in an open-backed truck, bringing Harry back to Hastings wrapped in a tarpaulin. There was no time for niceties in war.

Early on in 1950 the West Hill and District Association members had complained about the condition of the bombed sites in their area. Councillor W H Ruby said that there was space for 30 houses on the sites and their construction would clear up the disgusting places and he would put a motion to that effect to the council. The association members had expressed a complaint that was widely heard in the town about various bombed sites. So it was a relief when in September Hastings Council announced that the ban on building on bombed sites was removed, bringing an end to the freezing of work on the vacant lots. The ban had held up rebuilding on many sites, including London Road, St Leonards for five years, along with road-widening proposals. Councillor Rymill said that it would be years before the road scheme could be carried out and so the eyesores would have otherwise remained. Councillor A W Lennard said that Sidney Little’s scheme would never materialise. “It was only a brushed up job to bring Hastings to the forefront at the International Planning Conference at the White Rock Pavilion.”

1950

Aneurin Bevan, whom the Observer called the Father of the National Health Scheme, addressed a four-day conference for the Confederation of Health Service Employees at the White Rock Pavilion. Bevan emphasised that the public purse ought not to pay for every health idiosyncrasy:

Only that what medical science can give should be freely provided at the time it is needed...It would be a fundamental departure from the basic principles of the scheme if it was ever found necessary to charge for the National Health Service.

In the same edition of the paper Vigilant struck a timely note by reminding readers that after 1st October it would no longer be possible for a patient to automatically change to different doctor, except in the event of changing address. In April 1951 Bevan resigned from the cabinet over the planned charges for NHS teeth and glasses. He retired to the commons back benches, where he was joined by two other ministers, one of whom was Harold Wilson. This was a major blow to the stability of the Labour government, which had a very small majority.

The nation's butchers believed that they were the most put upon retailers during the long period of austerity. During their October trade conference in Hastings they sent a resolution to the Minister of Food declaring, "It is impossible for a butcher to make a fair profit on the present retail price of meat...We are being forced to sell B class meat to our customers at A class prices." It could not have helped when the butchers learned that at a meeting of the Hastings and St Leonards District Rabbit and Poultry Club its Chairman, Mr L A Eldridge had said, "Backyard farmers are producing 25% of the nation's eggs and their rabbits supply 30,000 cwt of meat per year. They are doing a wonderful job in helping the nation along." Mr Eldridge was therefore angry that the White Rock Pavilion management had refused permission for a rabbit show to be held in their lower hall because "rabbits are smelly". The management later relented.

Hastings Council said in late October that no effort was being spared to ensure that Hastings shared as fully as possible in the next year's expected tourist boom, engendered by the Festival of Britain. It was predicted that the national figure of 600,000 overseas visitors would increase to 700,000 due to the festival. Alderman Ford attended a meeting at the Travel Association Office to discuss the part that Hastings and other resorts would play in the overflow of London's visitors. He said: "We can only hope the lure of the seaside will triumph." Mr A K Vint, the Borough Public Relations Officer added:

Hastings will play a full part in welcoming overseas visitors to the Festival of Britain in 1951. Arrangements are already in hand to accommodate at short notice those who arrive without having booked rooms in hotels. Meanwhile, every effort will be made to make sure that Hastings is well known overseas.

Hastings Group Hospital Management Committee found a solution to a "vexed problem." A casual ward block at St Helen's Hospital was to be used as a temporary measure, to accommodate the town's evicted, homeless families and fit children, who were sent to the hospital by Hastings Council. Deprived and parentless children would be put in a children's ward in the same building; an arrangement that had echoes of the workhouse. At a cost of £1,200 a staff of five or six foster mothers and a cleaner would be provided at the expense of Hastings Council. The fourteen hospitals in the Hastings area had already cost £586,000 in the past year; the Group Finance Management Committee denied extravagance.

1951

On 6th January Hastings was informed that a visit was expected in May from Her Royal Highness Princess Elizabeth. Vigilant thought that the royal visit would be a tonic for winter-weary hearts and an intense pleasure. "It will give the town an ideal opportunity to demonstrate affection and admiration for the future Queen in this Festival of Britain Year." The council decided to spend £1,500 on painting up the town hall. The "bold plans" the council had drawn up for the Festival of Britain were made known: Illuminated fountains in Warrior Square, a floodlit, 20 foot high figure of a bathing belle at the bathing pool and an illuminated set piece of "Happy Harold", (the town's mascot) at the White Rock. The seafront flower beds were to be lit up and there would be festoons of coloured lights along the promenade. The estimated cost of this was £9,892. The still vacant bombed sites would be masked with six-foot high breeze block walls as wood for fences was in such short supply.

Major A Carlisle, DSO, MC of Fairlight Place made a gift to the town of 215 acres of cliff land and countryside to the east of Hastings that included Fairlight and Ecclesbourne Glens, a portion of Lovers' Seat on the cliff edge and the Dripping Well, at the head of Fairlight Glen. This gift increased to three and a half miles the tract of cliff land owned by Hastings Borough Council; described at the time as, "an area of scenery unsurpassed by anywhere on the south east coast."

Austerity-ridden Hastings residents had more basic things to concern them than fancy lights and beauty spots. In late January there was a further cut in meat ration; it was down to 4 ounces, the lowest it had ever been; thirteen people's ration books would have been required to buy a leg of lamb. Cooper-Key, Hastings' Member of Parliament, criticised the government on this subject saying that the people who are hard up are those who cannot afford to get a restaurant meal off the ration, as the Ministry of Food suggested they should do when their permitted rations were used up.

1951

February brought heavy rain and flooding to Hastings, the whole country experienced the wettest February since 1870; coal and coke prices went up as winter fuel shortages grew more acute. The flour situation had improved but in the spring the Ministry of Food announced higher prices for flour. Bakers were able to produce a greater range of cakes but had to increase prices, including that for the bread-round delivery charge, which went up to 3d per household.

A poster campaign to encourage locals to make the best of Hastings for the Festival of Britain was launched. Residents were asked to, "Paint your window boxes, install gay awnings and put up coloured lights, flags and bunting, to make Hastings and St Leonards the brightest spot on the south east coast." The plans for the expenditure on the part of the council were again met by the expected disapproval from correspondents to the Observer,

Dear Sir,
I fear that the distinct beauty and charm of the town will be lost in a miasma of ugly festoons. I also doubt that they will be of benefit to a substantial part of the community. Nor will it help the resources of the nation, for are we not still at war, in circumstances of peril and privation?
George G Herbert, Castledown House, Castledown Avenue, Hastings.

Vigilant later drew his readers' attention to the revival of the waste paper salvage scheme by Hastings Corporation and the plans to enter a national competition to become the town to collect the most waste paper; the contest was promoted by the Waste Paper Recovery Service. Vigilant enjoyed a good cause and this one seemed to take him back to wartime, when causes arrived on a weekly basis. He asked for a whole-hearted response from householders and traders. Newspapers, magazines and cardboard boxes were required for export, home consumption and defence purposes; it was to be presented to the dustman separated from other waste. The salvage scheme coincided with the installation of a new power press at the Hastings Corporation works yard; the machine compressed paper before it was sent to the mills. By the end of June paper to the value of £1,657 had been collected and after expenses had been deducted the balance was to go towards rates. The value of other salvage such as rags and metal was £510.

1951

Official respect for the town's historic architecture was legislated in March 1951 when the Listed Buildings Act came into force; 180 Hastings and St Leonard's properties were listed as places of local interest. These included the whole of Wellington Square and Pelham Crescent, Tudor Houses in the Old Town and Regency and early Victorian architecture in St Leonards and elsewhere. Designated buildings could not thenceforth be altered or extended without official sanction. Frederick Goodsell said in his leader article in the Observer:

This list, which appears to omit nothing of much merit, should afford great satisfaction to those who value the antiquities and charms of Hastings and St Leonards. It is of no use lamenting the mischief done during many decades but it is possible to learn something from these past mistakes... May the public grow more and more concerned to safeguard those buildings that give Hastings its enduring appeal and individuality among seaside residents.

The seaward end of the Palace Pier crashed into the sea in March during a fierce storm with gales of 70 mph, leaving only a few fragments of steel piles visible above the waves. Timber wreckage was washed up along the beach as far as Fairlight, providing firewood for early risers, before the corporation lorries appeared to clear the remainder. The demolition and removal of the pier, which was already underway, had been hastened.

April brought news that 20 of the 116 terraced houses planned at Hollington were already under construction, on sloping land with sea views, west of Hollington Rectory. This was the location of the bulk of the council's post-war building plans and its largest single housing unit. This site was chosen mainly because of the gentle land contours. The drop in level from one end of the site to the other being only 22 feet. Hastings Corporation announced that it was prepared to grant mortgages under the Small Dwellings Acquisition Act, to help people to buy homes. The maximum value of the house should not exceed £5,000 and the rate of interest was 3.25%. There were still 1,755 families on the local housing register.

On the 18th May came the highlight of the year - HRH Princes Elizabeth's visit; crowds of adults and school children turned out on a day of sun and cloud to give her a rousing welcome. The Princess wore a saxe blue fitted coat and matching frock, a close fitting felt hat trimmed with flowers to tone, navy blue shoes and gloves and triple strings of pearls. Young Hastings resident Moira Knight was allowed out from behind the counter of Alston's corset shop to stand in Robertson Street to watch the royal visitor pass by. Moira said, "Her skin looked like porcelain and her eyes were the most wonderful colour, like bluebells." Princess Elizabeth's visit lasted for three hours during which she embarked on a hectic programme of duties; laying the foundation stone of the bomb-damaged, newly restored St John's Church followed by lunch at the town hall. On the menu were cold salmon with cucumber and mayonnaise, grilled Tournedos Béarnaise, (in other words, steak in sauce) and Strawberries Parisienne with biscuits and coffee.

After lunch the Princess moved on to the grounds of Hastings Castle, where she was greeted by a party of fisherman who presented her with a gold winkle pin, a gift from the Old Town's Winkle Club. Princess Elizabeth admired the view from the castle ruins before being driven to the town centre cricket ground, overlooked by the castle and cliffs, where she received the deeds of Hastings Castle and those of the cliffs and glens of Fairlight and Ecclesbourne, handing them on to Hastings Mayor for safekeeping. Hastings Borough presented Princess Elizabeth with a souvenir of her visit; a silver replica of the town's 13th century corporate seal.

In her speech the princess said:

I pay tribute to the resolute spirit of Sussex when the danger of invasion threatened...I call upon the rugged battlements of the castle to serve as a reminder that the spirit of Hastings remained staunch and indestructible in spite of all the enemy could do against it...The beauty and heritage of the town must be guarded for future generations...I am glad to see so many children here today; the future is in your hands.

At the end of the ceremony Princess Elizabeth walked through an avenue of little girls, who scattered the grass with rose petals. Hastings was reluctant to let go of the magical atmosphere that the royal visit had engendered and for some weeks afterwards the paper featured readers' recollections of the royal visit. As Queen Elizabeth she returned twice to the town; in 1966 to mark the 900th anniversary of the Battle of Hastings and in 1997, to declare open the Priory Meadow Shopping Centre, built over the unique town centre cricket ground, where she had received the deeds of Hastings Castle.

Vigilant moved on to more mundane matters; late night buses:

I am pleased to note that the licensing justices have decided to grant later drinking hours in Hastings for the Festival of Britain season but will there be later buses to match these hours, to take home patrons and staff? We must also remember our Continental visitors, who do not understand our restricted licensing hours.

Three weeks later it was announced that four bus services would depart from the town centre at the later hour of 11pm.

In spite of the huge expenditure on festive lighting one visitor was not impressed:

Dear Sir
As a visitor to Hastings I must praise the flowers in the town's public gardens and parks. But I consider the illuminations for Festival of Britain Year a poor show, except for the pier display.
Miss E D Lea. Wales.

It's unlikely that this letter had any official influence but soon after its publication Councillor G Steele, Chairman of the Highways and Works Committee secured the town council's approval to the proposal to spend about £500 in improving Hastings' Festival of Britain illuminations. Vigilant pontificated on what he called "The ongoing conflict between the needs and wishes of residents and trippers".

There is a feeling among our townspeople that shop keepers concern themselves mostly with the needs of visitors, forgetful of the all-year-round custom provided by locals. With reference to the comic Saxon warrior illuminated sign at the approach to White Rock Gardens, Hastings needs to pay more attention to good taste than it has done in past years.

1951

Harry Henham, the first WWII soldier to be buried in the Hastings Cemetery Hero's Corner

Princess Elizabeth at Hastings Cricket Ground on the occasion of her 1951 visit to the town

1951

Hastings New Recycling Press

Sidney Little.
Hastings'
controversial borough
engineer

Sir Edward Hilton Young opens Hastings Promenade extension December 1931. Sidney Little stands front, extreme right

1951

He was pleased to report on 16th June:

Most people will be happy to learn that the floodlit Happy Harold picture at White Rock Gardens is to offend their sensibilities no longer. However, it was a wise decision that he will be retained as a trade mark in borough advertising material. The appearance of Happy Harold in the famous poster bearing the slogan "Hastings is Getting Ready for Your Invasion" was a first class publicity effort. But it should be remembered that recalling the 1066 era has only a limited usefulness in attracting visitors to Hastings. For such cheerful ugliness to predominate in the town's advertising may suggest that the graces of life are not to be found here. People who want the town to prosper should be increasingly mindful of those in their midst who cater for riff-raff." (The Happy Harold poster had been the winner of the Tattersall Trophy in 1949 for best resort poster in the country).

Vigilant closed this piece with a tilt at "vulgar postcards", possibly inspired by the following letter from a local reader:

Dear Sir,
Isn't it high time that the censors did something about the vulgar, suggestive and salacious postcards, produced in garish colours which are to be found so prominently displayed at many premises in the borough? It is horrifying to see young girls and boys studying these postcards, as do older people, who ought to know better and set a good example. The type of humour these cards exploit would never be allowed in the theatre or cinema."
Name and address supplied.

Vigilant's comments on Happy Harold and the content of the reader's letter are symptomatic of the snobbery and prudery that persisted in post-war Hastings. There were many like Vigilant, who wanted the town to epitomise "the graces of life", with Hastings perceived as a residential town that just happened to be a coastal resort. The more realistic understood that it would have to move with the times and embrace the "riff-raff". Hastings was at the peak of its post-war significance as a holiday destination; the cheap, continental package holidays and the use of the town as a dumping ground for the unwanted population of other towns and cities, changes that would seriously affect it as a seaside resort, were some years distant. For the 1951 August Bank Holiday the promenade was filled with seaside attractions for all ages; miniature trains, trams and coaches, a children's play land, an open air swimming pool and the White Rock Baths, There were twice-daily concerts on the pier bandstand and music and tea dancing in the Sun Lounge and White Rock Pavilion. Other more sporting attractions were a gymkhana, a water polo match and an aqua show. And, of course, all the traditional, glorious day trippers' pleasures of fish and chips, winkles and whelks, peppermint rock, paddling, funny hats and rude postcards, all the delight of the "riff-raff."

While visitors flocked to Hastings, its own residents had their eyes set on London and a trip to the Festival of Britain. To mark the festival every community throughout the land put on their own event, with pageants being the favourite choice but many art and design shows were held all over the country and 2,000 camp fires were lit across the country and Britain turned out in its millions to visit the Festival of Britain Exhibition. It was built on the Thames Embankment between Waterloo Bridge and the old County Hall, on 27 acres of war-damaged London. King George VI inaugurated the festival on May 4th 1951 saying, "We invite visitors from other lands to come and see what this old country can do." Initially proposed by the Royal Society of Arts in 1943, the Festival of Britain was intended to commemorate the centenary of the first world fair; the Great Exhibition of 1851. It was also hoped in 1951 that the festival would be a tonic to the nation and a symbol of faith in the future. In common with the more recent Millennium Dome, the Festival of Britain Exhibition was criticized by the press as a waste of money: The project's final cost was eleven million pounds; huge public expenditure in the time of food rationing, petrol shortages and the other effects of almost six years of war. Administrative resignations, strikes and wet weather plagued the exhibition's construction but in the end the public flocked to the attraction and it achieved an attendance of over 8 million, a figure that would be envied fifty years later by the organisers of the Millennium Dome, which attracted only 6.5 million visitors in the 12 months of its controversial existence.

The Festival of Britain Dome, four times the size of the Albert Hall was a massive inverted saucer-like building of aluminium that held, among many other exhibitions, a planetarium, a Polar Theatre featuring a life-sized reproduction of Captain Cook's ship Endeavour, and live huskies; a television pavilion that included Telecinema, where the audience wore special glasses to watch stereoscopic films. But for many it was the Festival of Britain's Skylon that captured the imagination. It was a slender, cigar-shaped sculpture rather than a building, apparently floating above the exhibition site. Supported on what looked like three slender legs, it was attached to a net of cables. It was unclear whether these supported its gravity-defying architecture, or anchored it to the ground. If the Skylon was an arresting sight by day it was even more exciting at night when a beam of light illuminated a structure that seemed to hold a promise of the space age yet to come. The festival was also a showcase for emerging trends in architectural and other forms of engineering and the use of new materials in building and it introduced fresh designs in furniture, ceramics, textiles, clothing, accessories and dress fabrics. These last three were seen by the visitors as luxury items, because they were in colours, designs and fabrics which for the most part had never been seen before. The sight of these desirable things was both an uplifting and depressing experience for austerity-hit Britons, as almost all the goods were destined for export only. To help rebuild the economy the Labour Government had been quietly trading these luxuries abroad in order to promote quality British goods. They achieved this by denying the British people access to them for as long as they possibly could. In 1951 Britain was in fact on the brink of becoming a huge consumer society.

The communal spaces on the festival site, laid out as a miniature city, were decorated with the work of famous sculptors. In the Minerals Pavilion, there was a mock-up of a coal mine, in the Countryside Pavilion tractors were displayed, rising and falling on hydraulic columns. Other festival exhibitions featured the sea and ships, homes and gardens, power and production. Boats ferried visitors from the two piers on each side of Hungerford Bridge to the Festival Pleasure Gardens in Battersea Park, where fun-fair rides, bizarre exhibitions, water gardens and regular firework displays delighted children and grown ups alike. There were many restaurants of modern and futuristic design on the exhibition site but the food, as might be expected of those austere times, is remembered as being universally bad. Sensible and thrifty visitors took packed lunches. The exhibition was not without its detractors and visitors complained of long queues, how badly dressed the British looked and the rubbish lying around. (All those packed lunches, no doubt)! The Festival of Britain closed, as planned, in September 1951.

In September came the announcement of an October General Election; the second in 19 months. Excitement ran high in Hastings' political circles; many were keen to see if the Liberal party's candidate in the 1950 election would stand again. Financial considerations were uppermost in the minds of the Liberal Association Committee when they gathered to discuss the situation. Their candidate, Peter Hurd was willing to stand; he had polled over 9000 votes in the previous election but the committee decided not to put him forward. Vigilant was of the opinion that most people in the Hastings constituency would prefer this: "They will be relieved that the Liberals are not contesting, leaving the way clear for a straight fight." Reflection on the local tone of the previous general election campaign may have caused Vigilant to comment, "I hope that political zeal will not develop into bitterness, wrath and evil-speaking." Vigilant later reminded his readers to send discarded election propaganda to salvage, "It is calculated that the paper used nationwide by the political parties would be enough to make half a million packing cases or plasterboard to line the ceilings of 12,000 new houses."

The Conservatives held Hastings with a 14,874 lead, returning Cooper Kay as the Borough Member of Parliament for the third time. The Labour vote for Mrs Catherine Williamson was increased by 2018 over the 1950 election. The voter turnout dropped from 82% in 1950 to 77% in 1951. The total votes cast for the two candidates were Conservative 34,495, Labour 19, 621. As the Conservatives returned to power and Churchill to Number 10, he promised to make Britain "strong and free". A twenty-six year old Conservative candidate, the youngest in the country, Miss Margaret Roberts, did not win in her constituency. The new Conservative Government demolished the Festival of Britain pavilions in 1952; only the Royal Festival Hall remains. Scandalously, the iconic Skylon was sold for scrap, as was the Dome of Discovery. In 1961 the site was developed as offices and car parks.

1951

As winter set in Doctor Parkman, the Borough Medical Officer, publicly deplored the state of some types of accommodation in Hastings:

The housing list remains painfully long...investigations by my department into the conditions under which families are living reveal truly heart-rending circumstances; overcrowding, structural defects, dampness, lack of facilities, no play space for children, either inside or out of doors. There are particular difficulties in the numerous basement and semi-basement flats. Many of these flats are in old buildings and in rooms that were intended for use as kitchen quarters. They are not fit for use as living or bedrooms and are most unsuitable for families with children.

In late November Plummer Roddis (now Debenhams) set up a show flat in their department store, displaying how it could be furnished for £426. The flat consisted of a lounge-diner, (not known as such in 1951) bedroom, sewing room and study. The dining table and six chairs on show were of a design exhibited at the Festival of Britain. The price included carpets, curtains and other furnishings. For buyers short of ready cash, Jay's Furniture, on the other side of the town centre, offered weekly terms for basic furnishing needs; a bedroom suite, consisting of a dressing table, chest of drawers and wardrobe, £36 (bed not included), three-piece suite, £27 and a dining table, four chairs and a sideboard, £29. At the start of December a delegation from the Hastings Town and Country Planning Committee went to London to visit the Ministry of Works. They were told that the priorities were for housing and rearmament and that there was little possibility of the building of shops or offices. The ministry said that it might be possible, in view of the detrimental effect of the town's appearance on visitors, to allow certain limited reconstruction of shops at London Road, St Leonards. Notification was later received that the ministry had issued a license for £1750, for the partial reconstruction of commercial premises at 7, London Road. Application was deferred on the building of two shops with flats or offices above at Swan Corner in Hastings Old Town; it was deemed more necessary and advisable to widen the road at Swan Terrace. As it transpired no building was ever erected on the vacant site where the Swan Inn once stood. It is now a garden of remembrance, dedicated to the many local residents who died in a Sunday lunchtime bombing raid on May 23rd 1943.

1952

Early in 1952 Hastings Borough Council published a report on town planning: Halton, classified as obsolete was to be demolished and an estimated 3000 houses were to be built throughout the town in the next 20 years. As well as 11 new schools there were to be new roads across the tram tracks at Bulverhythe and in the Bourne Valley, to by-pass the High Street. Also scheduled were road improvements at the Ridge from Ore to Fairlight, the extension of Blackman Avenue to Battle Road and traffic controlling improvements at the town centre. It was proposed that Wellington Square should be devoted entirely to offices and that obsolete property in Station Road, Middle Street and Priory Street should be pulled down and developed for offices and businesses. Industrial sites would be zoned at Ponswood Road and Caves Road, West St Leonards. There would be provisions for preservation of the Old Town and park-like areas in the borough; all projects having the aim of keeping Hastings as a seaside resort abreast with the times. The total estimated cost of the improvements, to be carried out between 1952 and 1956 was £560,000 per year; the money coming from a combination of Hastings Corporation, government departments and private enterprise. Most of these proposals were eventually carried out, not always in the manner planned and generally outside the ambitious time scale of four years. And of course, well over budget.

In a leader Editor Frederick Goodsell did not conceal his true feelings about the now retired Borough Engineer Sidney Little's previous plans for Hastings:

The present planning officer, Mr Baxter, has approached his task in a suitably cautious manner, very different from his sensational predecessor. The new plan contains none of the revolutionary proposals such as two-tier roadways, a subterranean bus station and the artificial lagoon, included by Mr Little in his earlier scheme for a future Hastings. We do not think the ratepayers will be sorry to hear the last of such awe-inspiring novelties, which would be out of place in a time of austerity. I am also glad that Mr Baxter has shown appreciation for the special character of the various parts of the borough.

The Hastings Borough Engineer Sidney Little made a huge mark on the town but almost nothing is said of Sidney Little the man. He was born in Carlisle in 1885, the middle child of three boys, whose father practised as a civil engineer and surveyor in Carlisle. After qualifying in his father's profession Little worked for the government during WWI on several construction projects, concluding his service with A V Roe, Aeronautical Engineers. After the war Little took the post as Ipswich Borough and Water Engineer and in 1922 married Angela; they had one child, a daughter, Jean. When Little came to Hastings to appear before the council appointments board for the post of borough engineer in 1926, he first walked about the town. He later said that he was dismayed by the neglect, decay and frowsy atmosphere of Victorian splendour that he saw. He is reputed to have told the interview committee Hastings needed to be dragged into the 20th century. That continued to be Little's attitude after his appointment; an appointment which he immediately regretted and tried to resign from but his resignation was not accepted. Little deserved his nick-name the Concrete King for more than disparaging reasons; he had a deep and practical knowledge of reinforced concrete and of the various uses to which he put the cement, taking his provenance from the Egyptian Pyramids to the Roman Parthenon. It also may have been contemporary Brighton that inspired Little to envision the future of a modern Hastings as a recreational resort. It should be remembered that the early years of Little's tenure in Hastings were during the economic depression and to his credit his modernising projects were instrumental in providing work for hundreds of local unemployed men.

As for the style of his avant-garde plans, the influences went far beyond the confines of Hastings and St Leonards. With feelings that another war was looming, nations began to reject everything that represented the old order, perceiving its attitudes as being responsible for the Great War. A social revolution was in progress, affecting attitudes to religion, politics, education and the class system as well as music, fashion and architecture. Buildings constructed up until the outbreak of the Great War in 1914 were frequently backward-looking in style, even if the methods and materials used in their construction were contemporary. The late 1920s and 1930s produced a new form of architecture, a startling departure from everything that had gone before. Generally known as Art Deco, it introduced a streamlined and geometric approach to design, reflecting an era that revelled in the machine. Art Deco buildings featured white rendered exteriors, clean lines, flat roofs; curved corners and windows, giving an impression of efficiency and modernity.

Little projected a dynamism that impressed; there was something of Napoleon about him. (We can only imagine the combined effects on his personality of his surname and being short in stature). It is said that he had an incisive, legalistic mind and a capacity for absorbing facts; he was able to make a case clear to himself and thereafter to any others he had to convince. He was a quiet man and never raised his voice and was described by those who knew him well as possessing courage, foresight and genius. He was courteous to women but did not encourage them to fill vacant posts in his department. He was known to be a devoted family man, his abiding interests being his garden and the Amherst Tennis Club, situated opposite to his house; he was president of the club all his life. In WWII Little served as Deputy Civil Engineer in Chief to the Admiralty and was in charge of defences at Scapa Flow and other bases. He was associated with the Mulberry Harbour scheme of prefabricated concrete D-Day Invasion ports. It is said that while Little was serving during the war Hastings Borough Council was re-structured and on his return to his post with the council he found his powers reduced, leaving him with no real chance of seeing through his grand plans for the town. One of Little's most influential critics was the local Architect Callow – but there is a time honoured antipathy between architects and engineers. Some of what Little did for or to, (according to one's view) Hastings and St Leonards would have come about in the normal course of progress – the increase in road traffic is an example. Little's present day detractors still have a strong voice, particularly in the Old Town, where the effects of his ruthless pursuit of the "City Beautiful", as he described his aspirations for Hastings, have left a damaged heritage. In 1960 Sidney Little was granted the Freedom of the Borough of Hastings for his promenade improvements; he died in April 1961.

Britain was still under food rationing in 1952, in fact new austerity measures were introduced by the government in January, which included more National Health Service charges. In late January the government announced that travellers would be allowed to take only £25 spending money abroad, with a view to encouraging holidays at home. Vigilant, of course, had an opinion:

Like all other resorts, Hastings can look forward to better business as the result of the government's decision to reduce the spending money allowance for foreign travel. It is known that France alone fears a loss in Sterling of about £10,000,000. Hastings Publicity Department should now make a feature of what it can provide for holiday-makers. In a letter to this paper last season a visitor called Hastings Lido-like and a pleasant alternative to a Continental holiday."

The sudden death of King George VI, aged 52 on 6th February, came as a profound shock to the nation, although the facts of his illness and treatment were well-known. The columns of the Observer's front page on 9th February were heavily bordered with black and the news of the King's death conveyed with great solemnity. Flags on all of Hastings public buildings and the fishing fleet were at half mast and the town was deserted and quiet. Places of entertainment were closed and there were mourning displays in shop windows; the BBC broadcast only news and solemn music. The local paper reminded its readers that in 1918 the King had stayed in Hastings, as Captain HRH Prince Albert; he was attached to a squadron of the Number 5 Wing Royal Air Force Cadet Brigade. Many local people could still remember the slim young officer they saw on formal and informal occasions in the summer of 1918; King George V made an official visit to Hastings on 30th August to review the brigade.

A Mr Guy Faraker wrote to the Observer challenging a reader's letter, which said that in 1918 as Prince Albert King George VI was billeted in a house in Sedlescombe Road North.

That is not quite correct. The prince's equerry, Wing Commander Greig rented the furnished house in question for himself and his family and His Majesty stayed with him there. I know this because I had the honour of negotiating the letting of the house to the wing commander, which brought me into contact with them both on numerous occasions.

1952

The King treated me with a friendly and unassuming manner and seemed to be a man of simplicity and kindness. On one occasion I was a passenger in a car he drove. The house where the King stayed was The Knoll, later known as Ledsham Court, in Harley Shute Road.

On 8th February the proclamation of the Queen's Accession was made by the Town Clerk, Mr N P Lester, from the steps of the town hall, at St Clements Church and in Warrior Square. In the Observer next day Vigilant was in historic mode.

Now that England is again reigned over by a Queen Elizabeth, it is worthy to recall that it was her illustrious predecessor of the same name who granted the borough its Charter of Incorporation...Under Queen Elizabeth II may Britain emerge from her difficulties to an era of prosperity, peace and happiness."

On the day of the King's funeral Hastings' mourning was focussed in a civic memorial service in St Clements Church. Shops and businesses were closed for at least part of the day and during the two minutes silence traffic came to a halt, post office telephone operators ignored calls, residents stood silent in the streets, where the only sounds were the cries of seagulls and the waves on the beach. In local schools the day was spent quietly, with services at the time of the funeral at Windsor.

In March the Hastings and St Leonards Hotels and Guest Houses Association was addressed by Mr H Harman, the resident director of the town centre department store, Plummer Roddis on the subject of "How to Judge a Hotel;

On entering the establishment if I am faced with a reception desk with a square of blotting paper that has not been changed for months I know full well what standard of service I will receive. Invariably there is a receptionist who has no welcome in her soul, who does not smile and has never been taught courtesy.

In a letter to the Observer a resident thought it would be a good idea if a certain local bank agreed to exchange its telephone number of 1066 with Hastings Information Bureau. "What splendid publicity would be given to a poster that said, "Spend Your Holiday in Hastings: Telephone 1066."

In mid-March, in a dispute over new conditions, drivers and conductors of the Maidstone and District Bus Company began to work to rule, declaring that they were prepared to keep it up for three months; the trolley buses ran normally. Vigilant came out fighting:

The only people concerned in the present bus dispute who are entitled to sympathy are the travelling public who are put to inconvenience enough by the work to rule and far greater by the Saturday suspension of services, cutting off visits for shopping and pleasure to people in the surrounding districts of Hastings and placing another burden on this hard hit town.

The drivers and conductors eventually won the dispute and the public were put to further inconvenience in September when bus fares were raised by 10% to cover the increased costs of wages and also fuel. On Thursday 29th May the Hastings Police conducted an experiment in traffic control at the town centre arousing much interest. Two constables on six-foot high control towers, placed at opposite sides of the Albert Memorial and facing east and west, directed the traffic by hand signals, while instructing pedestrians through loud speakers when to cross the road. It was thought that the flow of traffic was speeded up although there was a certain amount of confusion among the public and motorists when the experiment started; normally, five or six constables were required to control the point.

Sugar rationing was still in force, upsetting to people like my father who loved sweet tea. As we sat at meals on the farm at Fairlight, if his tea was not sweetened enough he would say to my mother, as a sarcastic hint, "Did you hear about that sugar boat that sank off Fairlight?" On 14th June the Glasgow steamer, "Baron Douglas", carrying thousands of tons of West Indian sugar, was badly holed in a collision during Channel fog. Four days later the vessel was beached near Gorse Cliff at Fairlight, where she lay half a mile off shore. Hundreds went to watch the rescue efforts but only a few spectators were present when the "Baron Douglas" was hauled off by tugs and taken to Tilbury. When the men working on the stranded vessel broke off for a cup of tea there was no sugar to be found on board so they had to get some from one of the tugs. Sea water entering a 55-foot gash in the side of the stricken vessel had ruined or washed away the 7,000 ton cargo of sugar; this represented one week's ration for 31,360,000 people.

The architect, Mr Callow made some ill-judged remarks at an enquiry concerning council house tenants that engendered fury in the aforesaid tenants. The nature of the comments can be gathered from a letter to the Observer dated 12th July headed "The Sunday Clothes Line."

Dear Sir,
With reference to Mr Callow's remarks at the Housing Site Enquiry about the Hollington football shirts, etc: If he would care to send me a cheque for approximately £30 for laundering we will ensure that what is obviously an eyesore to him on Sunday mornings is removed next season. Thanking him in anticipation.
J. T Marchant, Hon Sec, Hollington United Football Club, 4 Windsor Road, Hollington.

Coming to the defence of the Sunday laundresses and possibly seeing an opportunity to make a political point, the Hollington Labour Party Secretary wrote to the Observer the following week:

Dear Sir,
These good people do not do washing on Sunday because they like it but because they are busy during the week working elsewhere, to supplement their husbands' wages, which are admitted to be the lowest in the country. The high costs of living, rent, rates and taxes make it imperative that they should keep their heads above water. (A curious turn of phrase in the light of the letter's subject matter). *If this self-appointed critic thinks that they enjoy working like slaves he should think again.*
Mrs E N Hunt, Hon Sec, Hollington Ward Labour Party and E A D Cullen, Chairman.

A lively debate ensued from the end of July with the council's recommendation that the Albert Memorial Clock Tower be removed from Hastings Town Centre to ease traffic jams. After 19 speeches had been made Councillor Rymill said it was time for a vote; whereupon the council decided to defer taking any final decision on the memorial's future for three months, to give time for public opinion to be sought. The debate had arisen as a result of a report from the Highways and Works Committee which contained the resolution that the chief traffic obstruction was the clock tower and the committee recommended its removal. The Observer invited readers to express their opinion on the matter, using a cut-out form on its front page. Readers could select their response from three proposals: That the memorial should be removed completely, left untouched or removed to a better site. In a leader editor Frederick Goodsell commended the council for deferring a decision on the matter for three months; his own preference appeared to be that the memorial should be moved to another spot, perhaps only a few yards distant. He recognised that there would be no government grant for this choice:

To dismiss preservation of this famous clock tower as sentimental is to show a painful lack of appreciation for the strong feelings of the people who have, through bitter experience, grown sceptical of so called progress and understand it can be in a direction other than forward.

The following week the Observer's message was triumphant:

Let the Memorial stay, say Observer readers. The vote reflects the town's opinion – 1,264 have sent in forms marked in favour of retaining the Albert Memorial untouched and on its present site, 28 think it should be moved to a better site, 12 think it should be removed completely.

The poll was to run for a second week bringing the total of votes against the removal of the clock tower to 2,503 with only a total of 51 favouring the second and third alternatives. Letters poured in to the Observer not just from locals but from as far as New Zealand, Ceylon, Switzerland and Holland. Interest in the fate of the Albert Memorial was aroused nationally by a report in The Times, describing the public reaction to the Hastings Council debate. The letter column in the Observer printed 44 responses from readers, many suggesting different solutions to the traffic problems at the town centre; almost all of the correspondents were in favour of keeping the Albert Memorial.

1952

In mid-October the Town Clerk, Mr N. P Lester said:

It is not proposed to do anything at this stage which might involve the demolition of buildings. A temporary measure has been prepared to establish a different kind of island and to re-align the kerb so as to give increased traffic capacity. It seems that a time will come when something more substantial is necessary.

The "something more substantial" appeared in the late 1950s; a raised, grassy island was constructed round the Albert Memorial with the traffic flow organised to supposedly improve safety and avoid congestion. However, the new system often caused nervous pedestrians to take refuge on the grass. Pedestrian crossings were later installed but the layout still proved confusing, especially to overseas visitors. In April 1973 a fire occurred inside the clock tower; this was believed to be the work of vandals but no one was ever charged. In August 1973 the council announced its new plan for the town centre, deciding that the costs of repairs to the clock and the tower were not economic. To the dismay of local residents, the Albert Memorial was demolished in November 1973.

By the summer of 1952 there was a serious shortage of nurses, causing staffing problems at St Helen's Hospital and hindering surgeons in their work in August. Until this situation improved no more general surgical emergencies were to be admitted. Former Mayor, Mr Farnfield made an appeal to girls over 18 to consider nursing as a career as new recruits were urgently needed.

On 26th August thousands of holiday-makers and residents were shocked by the sudden and thunderous appearance of a secret aircraft in the skies above Hastings. They had experienced a preview of the de Havilland 110 Night and All-weather Fighter; the aircraft was set to give a display at the Farnborough Air Show the following week. There was a rush of complaints to Hastings Police and predictably, letters to the Observer:

Dear Sir,
Last Tuesday the peaceful pleasures of the people on the seafront were rudely shattered by the thunderous passage of a jet plane, tearing up

and down a few feet above the sea. I hope a repetition of the exercise will be prohibited by the authorities.
A E B.

Dear Sir
...The aircraft made a silent dive, only to open up right over the town with ear-splitting noise...To add insult to injury the pilot had the impertinence to do a final victory roll along the seafront! Can nothing be done to curb this menace?
W J Shorting, 5 Holmesdale Gardens, Hastings.

At the Farnborough Air Show on the 6th September thousands of spectators watched as a De Havilland 110 aircraft broke the sound barrier, disintegrated in the sky immediately above them and fell to earth. Thirty-one people, including pilot John Derry, were killed; dozens more were wounded. In the following week's Observer, published in its new, 12 page format, there was a small front page announcement. "There will be low-flying on Sunday 14th September in the Hastings neighbourhood between 12pm and 3pm. Unnecessary low flying is strictly forbidden but from time to time it is practised in authorised exercises." Hidden in the announcement one might find a vague apology for Hastings' dramatic introduction to what may have been its first sonic boom. Vigilant used the event to provide a timely reminder to readers to donate generously to Battle of Britain Week:

The Royal Air Force Association gives invaluable service to airmen, their wives and dependents when they are in need...We owe a debt to the RAF for its gallant defence of these islands in the dark days of 1940...We can show best that we have not forgotten their sacrifices by giving generously in the coming week.

In a letter that probably said more about the writer than the town, a man complained to the Observer: "My wife and I have lived in Hastings for 18 years and find it an unfriendly place. We have acquired no friends, only acquaintances and people who have spent their whole lives here could say the same." Vigilant leapt to the defence of the town in his Flotsam and Jetsam Column.

Sussex and Hastings folk are proverbially reticent and wary of strangers and not as forthcoming as those from other parts of the country; not unfriendly but reserved. But there is a tendency to cultivate friends in business circles and drop them when they have served a passing purpose. But when one looks at all the clubs and societies and the good works done locally the word unfriendly used of Hastings is not deserved. It must be remembered that nowadays hospitality costs money and Hastings people do not wish to reveal how frugally some of them live; they cannot afford to keep open house.

October 3rd 1952 saw the end of tea rationing: During a speech in Newcastle the Minister of Food, Major Gwilym Lloyd-George, said "Rationing and price controls on tea will be lifted; the government has taken advantage of a steady improvement in supplies of tea since the end of the war. The lifting of tea rationing follows Britain's recent re-entry into the international tea trading arena, with the resumption of public tea auctions in London." Nearly a third of the tea produced in the world was consumed in Britain and the government was no doubt hoping for a boost in popularity by making the nation's favourite beverage freely available again. However, a rush to buy tea was not anticipated, as the weekly ration had been increased to 3oz per head a week, the pre-war consumption level, some time previously. Meat was still rationed. The President of the local branch of the Meat Traders Association said to the 130 assembled members, at their annual dinner at the Royal Victoria Hotel, "Let us all hope that the day is not too far distant, when the task of the butchers will not be a misery of excuses and explanations, but a pleasure and a contribution to the well-being of British family life." He was referring to the meagre rationing system still in place six years after the official end of WWII.

The Old Hastings Preservation Society was launched on 22nd November 1952 at a crowded meeting held under the chairmanship of the Mayor H W Rymill, at the Hastings Old Town Branch Library. The object of the society was declared to be and remains the preservation of the antiquity and character of the Old Town, to arouse appreciation of its history and institutions, to preserve its ancient monuments and oppose harmful developments. Vigilant was delighted:

We now have body in existence capable of speaking in clear and informed accents for our picturesque Old Town, a treasure not to be lightly tampered with.

The Old Hastings Preservation Society went on to be a major force in the protection of a number of important buildings and features in Hastings. Examples are:

The black, tarred net huts on the Stade and the nearby Fishermen's Church, now a museum.

The Hastings fishing boat, the Enterprise, was made the centrepiece of The Fishermen's Museum. An OHPS committee oversees the running of the museum; it is said that it is the second most popular visitor attraction in the region after Leeds Castle.

The OHPS also preserved the Georgian stables at the northern end of the High Street. The building, now the Stables Theatre, has been described as one of the finest examples of Georgian domestic architecture.

The Old Hastings Preservation Society's biggest campaign was to rescue from decay and dilapidation St Mary in the Castle Church, built into the living rock of Hastings West Hill cliffs. The OHPS received support for this endeavour, both financially and by patronage, from Her Majesty Queen Elizabeth the Queen Mother and Sir Winston Churchill.

Signs of the turning of the tide of austerity were to be found in the pages of the mid-December Observer; the newsprint seemed to be of slightly better quality, the photographs sharper and its size was increased to 16 pages - the biggest edition since wartime cuts took over. Most remarkable of all was the inclusion of colour, albeit just red, on the pages advertising a wide range of Christmas gifts; goods which for the war years had been in short supply or unobtainable.

1953

A news item on 10th January 1953 said that growing unemployment in Hastings was becoming a serious problem; there were 1,635 on the list, the highest figure since the war. Lack of work off-season contributed to this figure, as in most holiday resorts. At a public meeting on the subject, convened at Hollington Junior School by Councillor D B Theaker, a proposal was approved that consideration should be given to asking the government for a grant for relief funds through the agency of the local employment committee or the town council. The sum of £5000 per week was already being spent on unemployment pay and National Assistance in the area.

From the summer of 1952 the Observer had been publishing news items about Hastings' plans for the coronation but the turn of the year brought a new impetus to preparations as well as considerable speculation as to what the new Elizabethan age might bring. In January Vigilant made a jaundiced review of the sentiments he had expressed shortly after the death of King George in 1952 when he had said, "Under Queen Elizabeth II may Britain emerge from her difficulties to an era of prosperity, peace and happiness".

In sterner mode in 1953 he wrote:

I cannot go all the way with some of the highfalutin pronouncements on the new Elizabethan age that we hear and read now. It is all too easy to draw misleading comparisons and raise false hopes, just because two Queens of England, separated by 400 years, bear the same name.

After a considerable amount of pulpit rhetoric Vigilant concluded:

Surely it should be a source of inspiration to us all to see a young Queen, all too soon called to bear vast responsibilities.

1953

The Old Hastings Preservation Society, inaugurated in November 1952, with a membership of 83 had increased this figure to 150 by January 1953, with the hope of having 1,000 members as soon as possible. The society made a statement to the Observer:

Any new development or reconstruction affecting the Old Town that is brought to our notice will be considered from the point of view of preserving the town's character; we shall act whenever danger threatens. Recently some of the trees in the Wilderness (a now vanished wooded and walled garden at the northern end of the High Street) *have been marked with paint. We are determined this will not mean their death warrant without a full statement of the grounds of such action.*

To mark the coronation the OHPS planned to organise, "Drawing room talks, sponsored by well-wishers, in order inform overseas visitors about our glorious heritage of ancient buildings and historic associations." In a move to preserve the Old Town Net Shops and as a result of meetings between the fishermen and the Highways Works Committee it was agreed to recommend to the town council that the ground leases of the net shops that were let to registered fishermen would not be decided for the next ten years. In nine instances where the officially-styled "rope shops" were not used in connection with the fishing industry the committee recommended that the tenancies should be terminated and the net huts let out to registered fisherman, who would be selected by the Fishermen's Society.

There was no big rush on sweet shops as the rationing of confectionary came to an end for a second time on Thursday 5th February. Trade was reported as brisk, one shopkeeper describing it as being like a busy Saturday. There was no panic buying as seen in the April 1949 lifting of rationing of sweets as stocks were plentiful. One Old Town trader put a notice in his window – "Freedom at Last!" This second de-rationing of sweets eventually had a dramatic effect on the industry; spending on confectionary increased by about £100 million by 1955, making history in the trade. The nation now spends over £5.5 billion each year on confectionary.

Vigilant was taken up with matters architectural on 14th February. He was pleased to note that rebuilding had started on some of the more prominent bombed sites in the borough and that on others preliminary clearance was underway. Along with these observations Vigilant gave a summary of a long letter of explanation for the years of delay in rebuilding, which he had received from the Hastings Town Clerk; as is frequently the case with such documents, it made tedious reading. It was the subject of the rebuilding in the Old Town that excited Vigilant's imagination:

Tudor-style reconstruction with touches of Gothic, have transformed the sea-end of All Saint's Street. Conversion of other derelict buildings has also been carried out or is in prospect. I am aware that the picturesque restoration has provoked more than one architect to express cautious criticism but the new work is in its way quite delightful and a real improvement. I would rather see the Tudorbethan dwellings recently completed in All Saint's Street than the utility façade of the new houses at Hastings Wall or the garden city type of building put in the Bourne before the war.

A correspondent to the Observer was less inclined to compromise:

Dear Sir,
As an ex-resident I must protest at the so-called restoration of certain houses in the Old Town: On a recent visit I was appalled to find the lower end of All Saint's Street transformed into something resembling Walt Disney's Snow White and the Seven Dwarfs. The olde oake beames associated with roadhouse architecture of the 1930s are much in evidence. Surely the local authorities have the power to prevent the Old Town from becoming a Tudorbethan desert?
James Wyatt. AA Dipl: ARIBA. 30 White Horse Drive, Epsom

Snobbery about mock-Tudor had been intense for years, ever since the genius cartoonist Osbert Lancaster attacked what he described as Roadhouse and Stockbroker's Tudor in his book Pillar to Post, published in 1938. The house to which Vigilant and Wyatt particularly refer is Pulpitt Gate, which stands at the sea end of All Saint's Street. An Old Hastings Preservation Society booklet informs that the house is named after the small postern gate that was once nearby in the town wall. Despite its appearance to the contrary the house is mainly a modern creation, having been built in 1953 using old materials. Its impressive southern window came from Lord Brassey's home, Normanhurst at Catsfield.

The death of Queen Mary, the grandmother of Queen Elizabeth, occurred on 25th March 1953, a loss that was echoed fifty years later when the Queen's mother died at almost the same interval before the marking of the Golden Jubilee. Frederick Goodsell's leader was suitably solemn:

...We share the widespread and sincere sorrow at the news of the death of her Majesty Queen Mary...In a world of change and unrest she represented the stability and serenity of high principled conduct...

Flags on Hastings' public buildings flew at half mast, tributes were paid at social functions and meetings and one minute silences observed. The Observer cast round for Queen Mary connections with Hastings; they were fleeting, to say the least.

While Queen Mary was staying at Compton Place at Eastbourne with King George V in 1935 she paid two visits to Hastings: Accompanied by the Princess Royal she was driven along the seafront; two days later she passed through the borough when returning from a visit to Rye and Winchelsea. She was met at the boundary by a police motorcycle flying squad. Queen Mary expressed a wish to visit the Old Town; her car drew up outside Gallops the ship's chandler in Rock a Nore Road and a lady in waiting alighted to buy a small, white wicker shopping basket.

On the 1st April, for the benefit of the Observer photographer, the Hastings Head Postmaster put a letter into the first post box in the town to bear the insignia ER II. It was installed at the Clive Vale Post Office in Mount Road. The public was informed:

The post boxes that bear the insignia of previous monarchs will only be replaced as they wear out and it is unlikely that Hastings will receive any more ER II boxes for some time.

The fact that there was a national scrap metal drive in progress hints at it being a very long time indeed.

1953

The nation seemed to view the forthcoming coronation festivities as marking the official end to austerity and the arrival at last of the promised "broad sunlit uplands" of Winston Churchill's Finest Hour speech of June 1940. In Hastings, Coronation Day started with a bang, when the maroon that calls out the lifeboat crew was fired in a 5am salute in overcast and damp weather that continued all day. The early awakening, which did not please everybody, signalled the start of 18 hours non-stop celebrating in the Old Town. There were street games – including a tug of war, a balancing baskets race and a challenge to eat treacle-coated buns suspended on string. Afterwards the faces of the contestants were pushed into a bath of bran. The men seemed to think that the idea of the game was to get as messy as possible; Bunk Harffey suffered a tin of treacle being emptied over his head. The tradition of humiliating forfeit-type games still lives on in the Old Town; contemporary fund-raisers in the Old Town Week Pram Race have been splattered with a soup of raw fish guts or baptised with cold porridge.

For one young mother Coronation Day became unforgettable for personal reasons: Mrs Marie O'Neill, of 3b Carisbrooke Road, gave birth at home to twins, a boy and a girl at 12.45am. The parents decided to christen them Norma Elizabeth and Norman Phillip, in honour of the day. It was believed at the time that they were the first twins to be born in Britain on Coronation Day; their birth was something of a shock to the parents as they had made preparations for only one baby. They later wrote to the Observer to "Express our appreciation to the kind people who have given or offered us assistance and the many nice presents we have received for the twins."

A Coronation Pageant took place in front of a crowd of 9,000 in Alexandra Park. The Mayoress, Mrs Rymill, had to stand in for her husband at the park and all other public events on Coronation Day – two of the Hastings Cinque Port Barons were invited to witness the coronation; one was the Mayor, Alderman Rymill and the other Alderman H Burden, senior serving ex-mayor; in all 18 seats were allocated to representatives of the Cinque Ports. At least 14 coronation street parties for children were organised in Hastings and St Leonards but the weather, which by the afternoon had settled into a relentless drizzle, drove many inside, one party took place in a garage; the 90 children at Saint George's Road decamped to the Mendem Hall. The Greville Road Street party, held on the Friday before the coronation, enjoyed brilliant sunshine. Tables that had been dragged into the street were set with red, white and blue decorations, summer flowers and paper plates; each child took their own cup and spoon. The festive tea was declared open by the Rev R B Finn and the children enjoyed sandwiches, biscuits, lemonade and ice-cream. The mayor and mayoress paid a visit; Sandra Ballard and Robert Newton presented Mrs Rymill with a bouquet. After tea there was a fancy dress competition, judged by Mrs Vast and Mrs Morris, followed by games, races and community singing. Every child went home with gifts; a bag of sweets, a coronation mug and propelling pencil or a mug and spoon. A commemorative book was presented to every Hastings schoolchild; it was "Elizabeth Our Queen" by Richard Dimbleby, the BBC's commentator on momentous state occasions. A foreword by Mayor Rymill said:

I am delighted to write a foreword to this book which is given to you as a coronation souvenir...I am sure you will be especially interested in the picture of our Queen when she visited Hastings and the children gathered together to show their affection and loyalty to her Royal Highness.

Reception of the coronation TV transmission in Hastings was good, the Observer reported:

At the Royal Victoria Hotel history was made; Rediffusion Ltd provided the establishment with 17 television sets. In the Oak Room 11 were installed with a large audience in attendance. There are plans for this new TV relay service to be pushed forward in the town at all speed.

Vigilant was in sunny mood when commenting on coronation events:

I commend the good work of the Mayoress Mrs Rymill and the capable and charming way she carried out her duties." Mrs Rymill had attended 14 separate events on Coronation Day between the hours of 8.15am and 10.15pm. Vigilant continued: "My television viewing on the outskirts of the borough was perfect, disturbed only by interference from the occasional passing car. I appeal to all car owners to have a suppressor fitted; it is a real piece of good neighbourliness.

He added a tribute to the "generous owners of television sets", endorsing the view expressed in a reader's letter. It appears that in 1953 television owners were regarded as the butt of humour, as we read below:

Dear Sir,
TV owners may appear as a joke for the cartoonists but there were many people who were grateful to those owners who shared with others their pleasures on Coronation Day. My own neighbours, who are strangers to me, asked me and a dozen others to spend seven hours viewing with them. They provided us with food and drink and I would like to say thank you to my neighbour.
Mr Ernest Mogg, Winchester House St Leonards.

To celebrate the coronation everyone was allowed an extra 1lb of sugar and 4oz of margarine for the month of June. The de-rationing of eggs in March and of cream in April may have prompted even the meanest of neighbours to feel hospitable. Millions of people all over the world saw the coronation live on television. This author went to Guestling Village Church with her boyfriend; we watched the coronation on a projector screen that was set up in front of the altar while we joined in the televised service's hymns and prayers. In the late afternoon we went to London, where we struggled down the jam-packed Mall until we were squashed against the Buckingham Palace railings. To the crowd's chant of "We want the Queen" she appeared on the balcony; a tiny, robed figure but even from that distance the flash of the jewels in the crown could be seen.

Reports from Hastings people who had been to the coronation appeared in the Observer the following week; all were impressed with the magnificence of the occasion, the precisely-planned arrangements and the speedy solution of unforeseen disasters. Hastings Mayor Alderman Rymill was accommodated in a hotel the night before the coronation:

We went to bed early but it was impossible to sleep. There were the

1953

Pulpitt Gate House. A 'Tudorbethan' reconstruction in Hastings Old Town

Coronation Street Party in Greville Road

1953

The 1953 Carnival Queen and her princesses

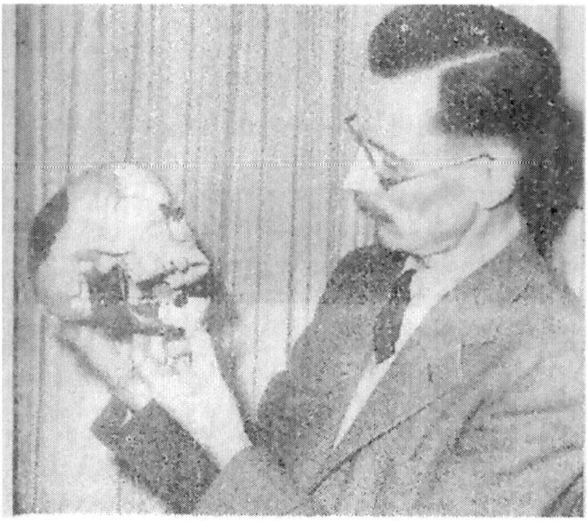

Hastings Museum Curator, John Mainwaring Bainees holding the museum's cast of the Piltdown Man Skull

sounds of barrel organs, accordions and singing in the street and the continual tramping of feet the whole night through. We had tea at half past three and breakfast at 5am. There was a problem about our transport to Westminster Abbey but it was quickly and discreetly solved. We arrived in our seats in the abbey at 7am and settled down to wait four hours, watching the arrivals of important guests and dignitaries. I noted that Winston Churchill was wearing beneath his mantle of the Order of the Garter the uniform of the Lord Warden of the Cinque Ports. I was deeply moved by the solemnity and beauty of the coronation service.

Hastings Chief of Police, Lt Colonel Cargill was present on the coronation procession route. Near where Cargill stood was a young American reporter, crouched over a typewriter on the pavement. In drizzling rain he noted his impressions of the procession and crowd scenes in extravagant prose. A group of 17 Hastings police officers had travelled to the capital on May 31st to represent the borough force at the coronation. The men were accommodated under canvas at Kensington Gardens and the only female police officer in the group, Miss Ethel Tucknott, stayed in a police section house in Bayswater. They returned on 3rd June, all feeling it had been a great honour. Ten students, six girls and four boys, from the Hastings Hotel and Catering School were sent to London to serve coronation guests. The students reckoned that between them they had waited on about 10,000 people at one time or another. In one marquee there was such a crush that some shelves collapsed; the police were called and services were suspended for half an hour till order was restored. Among the Hastings students was Jill Rowland aged 19, who said that she had waited on Winston Churchill, the Commonwealth Prime Ministers and many other distinguished guests who were part of Queen Elizabeth's Coronation Procession.

Hastings held its annual Carnival Week in the first week of July; the theme of the Coronation Year's procession was Happy and Glorious. Vigilant expressed his thoughts on "The Big Carnival Procession":

Nine out of ten people who had watched it thought it fell flat and below last year's standard; too many trade exhibits and too many queens. Well, this is Coronation Year and we could expect an extra touch of regality. However, the striking build-up of cars advertising national products certainly tended to overshadow the homemade entries from local societies. I think that although a carnival procession needs to contain no grim reminders of war, past or present another military band or two would be most welcome. The incongruity of the carnival queen's float being drawn by a tractor, bright and shiny as it was, struck many onlookers. A horse-drawn coach is the ideal equipage for royalty in procession; carnival royalty being no exception.

The usual programme of carnival week events took place, including a baby show. Among the successful contestants were the coronation twins. A surprise item in the show was the presentation of a grey twin pram and a case of baby food to Mr and Mrs O' Niell. This gift was in appreciation of the parents for bringing the town so much national publicity on the birth of the only twins in the country on Coronation Day. (The twin's first birthday was marked by a photo in the Observer; the babies had received many cards and gifts, including two silver five shilling pieces, (25p) one of which was of special interest to their father, a GPO night telephonist. The coin was dated 1884, the year the first message was sent by telegram). It was customary for a Royal Navy vessel to be anchored off Hastings during carnival week. In 1953 a change to the custom found the United States Warship "Zellars" off-shore. Although bad weather kept the American crew on board for part of the visit, when they came ashore the men were greeted by the local girls with the same enthusiasm that had met their compatriots some ten years previously. The town ran out of its stock of tartan and tweed fabrics, Devon fudge and all other things considered British by the Americans, for gifts to the folks at home.

After the carnival, the "pantomime": The following week Hastings Magistrates' Court heard a case against four local traders, instigated by a visitor, Mr Wellman of Finchley Road, London. He had purchased 12 comic postcards in Hastings with the purpose of making a legal point. He took the cards to the police station and lodged an official complaint about their content; the police said they were obliged to follow it through; giving the impression that it was with reluctance. Mr R T K Perkins, the defending solicitor for the traders brought before the court said that the cards were "A traditional part of the English seaside resort." The traders had been summoned for "Exhibiting for sale certain indecent cards contrary to section 224 of the Hastings Improvement Act 1885." Deliberations kept the court occupied for two hours, deciding as to whether the cards were indecent or not. Of Mr Wellman it was learned that he was an Evangelist who did not drink or smoke or go dancing. He said in court, "I believe there are dangers in certain types of dancing such as jiving, where women are put upside down." He had a sympathiser in Vigilant who wrote yet again that he thought it was time to clean up the comic postcards displayed on racks outside the shops:

Once upon a time the humour on these cards was vulgar without being suggestive; nowadays viscous innuendo has been creeping in to an extent which the broadest of minds could scarcely regard as healthy. Traders should get together to operate some unofficial form of censorship.

The traders involved in the comic postcards case were each fined £2 with £1-11- 6d (£1.60) costs.

Many of the cards seen outside the Hastings and St Leonards shops were by Donald McGill, surely the best remembered postcard artist of his time. Contrary to the public's expectations he was a bookish, amiable man, who looked like a small town solicitor, living his entire life in the London suburbs. McGill never became rich; he was paid a one-off fee for each postcard design and received no royalties from their astronomic sales, leaving only £735 in his will. Between 1904 and his death in 1962, he devised and drew an estimated 10,000 original cards, which have become part of our graphic heritage. The cards sold in their scores of millions, perpetuating a music-hall world of comic clichés: henpecked husbands, fat, jolly ladies, red-nosed drinkers, disapproving clergymen, busty barmaids, frustrated spinsters, lecherous milkmen and mean Scots. In July 1954 McGill, then almost 80, appeared before Lincoln Quarter Sessions to face charges under the Obscene Publications Act.

Two examples of the postcards in question were:

Flighty girl to bookmaker at racecourse: "I want to back the favourite, please. My sweetheart gave me a pound to do it both ways."

1953

A cheery male seaside tripper on the beach depicted holding an outsize stick of skywards-pointing seaside rock between his knees. The card's caption asked, "A stick of rock, Cock?"

McGill was advised to plead guilty on six counts, and was fined £50 with costs. The law had judged that six comic seaside postcards would deprave and corrupt the population.

During the summer of 1953 midnight bathing was re-introduced and the Daily Sketch printed a photo of the event which reveals a remarkable contrast between the half-naked youngsters struggling to throw a girl in the sea and the staidly dressed onlookers, complete with hats, handbags and pearls, looking as if they might have been chaperones. An end-of-season report said that the influx of visitors arriving by car was the greatest since before the war and seasonal hotel bookings were up on the previous year. A drop in the number of day trippers was put down to the counter-attraction, provided by the coronation in June; the month that traditionally brought factory and school coach outings to the town. However, Hastings had never before experienced so many overseas visitors, mostly from the Continent; this was ascribed to a special publicity campaign carried out in 1951. It was concluded that Hastings had held its own as a resort in a difficult year.

Vigilant turned his attention to the Hastings housing problem and the deterioration of the town centre:

The council should give encouragement to the re-development of existing properties so that the outward sprawl of new buildings may be kept within reasonable bounds. One big set-back encountered in converting houses into flats arises from the fairly recent regulation on fire escapes, a costly item that deters many owners. Hastings Local Authority might like to take the lead in pressing the government to institute a grants system to help property owners in this matter, thus saving Central Hastings from lapsing into blight because of the high cost of conversion.

The town centre Havelock Road bombed site was still undeveloped, as were others equally prominent, giving the town a snaggle-tooth look.

1953

A scientific scandal made front page news on the Observer on 28th November 1953; the famous Piltdown Man skull was a forgery. The local news focussed attention on the person most closely associated with the skull, a solicitor, Mr Charles Dawson, whose parents once had a house in Warrior Square, St Leonards. In his youth Dawson was articled to Hastings solicitor Mr F A Langham. Dawson took a great interest in Hastings; he wrote a history of its castle and later became known for doing much to benefit his local community, but he is best remembered today as the discoverer of the "Piltdown Man", named after the spot in Sussex where the bone fragments were unearthed in a gravel pit by workmen. The discovery was hailed in its time as the proof of an evolutionary "missing link" between apes and man. On the 22nd November The Times published findings by the Department of Geology at the British Museum and the Department of Anatomy at Oxford University: "While the fragments of the Piltdown cranium are genuine remains of a primitive man the large fragments of the jaw and the separate canine tooth are actually those of a chimpanzee, deliberately faked to simulate a fossil." Thus the Piltdown man was proved to be a forgery and a hoax, which some anthropologists had suspected since its discovery. There has been much discussion since 1953 about who was the actual hoaxer; debate has swung for and against Dawson as the perpetrator, the current opinion being that it was he. Other names suggested have been the Sussex-dwelling writer, Sir Arthur Conan Doyle, Teilhard de Chardin, the priest, biologist and palaeontologist, who resided at the Jesuit College at Ore Place, on The Ridge, Hastings and Dawson's friend, Arthur Smith Woodward, Keeper of Geology at Natural History Museum. Various researchers who suspect Dawson as the culprit, remark on his revealing tendency to speak about his discoveries directly to the press before, or even as an alternative to, publishing in academic journals and his habit of making dubious claims about his various discoveries. One of these was a Roman iron statuette, found at Beauport Park on the Ridge in 1877. In 1893 the Society of Antiquities dismissed the statuette as a modern iron copy of a tourist souvenir, probably based on a Roman original. Dawson admitted some years later it had been found in a cinder heap. As a result of the exposure of the Piltdown Man fraud, text books would need to be re-written. Charles Dawson, who had achieved international recognition as the greatest British antiquarian and amateur palaeontologist, died in 1916, long before the fraud was exposed.

1953

Vigilant added a touch of vinegar to his pre-Christmas column:

I have observed a pleasant increase of the custom, common in Germany and America I believe, of having an illuminated Christmas tree in the front window of the house, so that passers by may enjoy its charm; I have never seen so many lighted Christmas trees before; nor heard so few juvenile carol singers at the door, which gives me great satisfaction.

Vigilant, a lover of classical music had no time for untrained public singing. In 1945 he complained about people singing in pubs:

I have commented previously on the curious fact that in this country, music and alcoholic refreshment often lead to disharmony, and not solely in the musical sense. Hours of maudlin wailing take place in some public houses, to the distress of the licensee and his customers, who would gladly accept a ban on spontaneous vocalism; music can inflame as many breasts as it soothes. In these days of endless radio crooners, people can do without this noise when they drop in for a friendly glass.

1954

The winter of 1947 is often recalled as the coldest of the period; it was certainly protracted but 1954 was a good match for temperature. "The lowest recorded since the local weather station opened in 1947." said the Borough Meteorologist, Mr J V Taylor. On Thursday 28th January easterly winds sweeping down from Scandinavia brought to Hastings a bitter cold that froze even the salt water in the Marina outdoor bathing pool; the ice had to be broken up to prevent pressure causing damage to the pool surround. One of the coronation swans, a gift to Alexandra Park, was frozen into a lake and would have died had not a passer-by called a park attendant to release the bird. A thaw set in very quickly only for the north east winds to return bringing the lowest temperatures for seven years, causing widespread havoc in the town. There were over 1,000 cases of domestic burst pipes and associated problems and 31 accidents on the icy streets. Schools were closed and 350 street stand pipes were installed to enable frozen-up householders to draw water. Three houses caught fire as a result of plumbers misusing blowlamps to unfreeze pipes. One fire at 35 Fellows Road spread to the adjoining property; after the fire brigade had put out the fire and made the scene safe they found that their hoses had frozen solid.

Hastings Hospital Management Committee agreed to certain economy measures to limit the cost of a proposed new outpatients department to £70,000, to avoid any further delay of the construction of an extension to the Royal East Sussex Hospital. The new work was to get underway in April. The new department would be connected to the main hospital by a two tier-corridor. The RESH fell into disuse after the opening of the new Conquest hospital on the Ridge and was eventually demolished to make way for houses.

In early February Hastings Borough Council issued a leaflet to encourage owners of older properties to take advantage of new housing improvement grants, explaining that it was not a loan but a gift that did not have to be repaid, unless the reasonable conditions attached to the loan were broken. Sums from £150 and up to not more than £800 per single house or flat were available. Payments up to £3,200 would be granted in the case of a house converted into four flats or to bring a property up to date by installing a bathroom and a hot and cold water system or similar type of improvement. In topical vein Vigilant commented at length on the inadequacies of British plumbing and put forward a suggestion by a Swedish journalist, which he had read in the national press; that some kind of drinkable anti-freeze could be added to the domestic water supply to prevent burst pipes! He moved on to a report on the holiday market issued by the British Travel and Holidays Association:

We may elicit from the report the fact that more people went on holiday last year and gave resorts their best season in terms of numbers since 1949. But money was tight and few resorts could report a proportionate increase in spending. The number of people who took holidays on the Continent increased by 15% compared with 1952.

Vigilant was also pleased to record:

The flourishing state of the Old Hastings Preservation Society, which was reflected in the large attendance at the meeting held at the town hall on 12th February. Chairman Philip Cole said that the society had achieved its first principle object; that of securing the cooperation of the town council and the town's people as a whole.

Membership of the OHPS stood at 381, a good increase on the 83 enrolled at the inaugural meeting in November 1952.

In March Hastings Education Committee decided that the old stables at the top of the Hastings Old Town High Street were not suitable for adaptation as the School of Art. There was concern recorded by the Old Hastings Preservation Society, meeting elsewhere on the same night, of "The possibility of this Georgian building of excellent design ceasing to exist." Vigilant opined:

Most people would consider that the education committee had turned down a cheap and happy solution to the problem and instead has turned its thoughts to a new college of further education. The loss of the stable buildings would be irreparable. The town cannot afford to lose any more of its remaining artistic assets. To put them to cultural use turns them from museum pieces into rewarding factors in the day-to-day life of the borough.

In May 1954 the Observer reported: "Large groups of Dutch and German school children visited Hastings and were present at the mayor-making ceremony at the White Rock Pavilion." For decades this event has been an opportunity to show off the town's quaint, official functions to foreign visitors. In the early 21st century the ceremony was enlivened by a former town councillor with a personal grudge, who mounted the steps of the theatre's stage and struck the incoming mayor on the face with a glove, shouting, 'You have insulted my wife!' The party of French guests, who are mentioned in the local newspaper as being present, must have been either bemused or enchanted by this archaic gesture, possibly thinking it part of the ceremony. The White Rock Pavilion was also the scene of a case of overseas student misbehaviour in 1954: In a news brief the Observer noted;

Fifty French students were banned from attending a Humphrey Lyttelton jazz concert held there because of previous noisy behaviour at jazz concerts. Bandleader Ambrose, at an earlier concert, told students to shut up, after they had been whistling, stamping and shouting during the performance. Students were also criticized by young locals for jiving during dances at Hastings Pier, something local youngsters were banned from doing.

It was in 1954 that the student industry, as it is known today, began to burgeon. Shortly after the ending of the war the arrival of visitors to Hastings from the Continent began; numbers were increased by the establishment of the Twin Towns Scheme in 1948 but these were insignificant compared to the millions of students who would stay in Hastings over the next half century. The criticism by 'young locals' of the behaviour of students was a symptom of the animosity that was already appearing on the streets. Ex-Police Inspector Banks, a host-father for many years, said:

In the early 1950s foreign students from former enemy countries suffered some hostility from British teenagers; assaults and robberies became fairly frequent and required special attention from the police. Some years later it became customary for the student agencies to provide their students with distinctively patterned haversacks and this practice provided an easy means of identifying the agency responsible for the students and unfortunately picking them out as targets for violence. I recall some difficulties arising from foreign students refusing to queue properly at bus stops and several cases arose from them being roughly handled in consequence. From the 1950s onwards the fees paid to local householders for the accommodation of students became an essential factor in improving the local economy and in many cases maintained solvency. The total of the local unemployed was depressingly high and the town's economy was only very slowly recovering from the effects of WWII.

The Queen and the Duke of Edinburgh returned from their six month tour of the Commonwealth on 15th May 1954. During their passage home the yacht Britannia and her escort sailed up the channel, passing Beachy Head at midnight before docking in London. In honour of the event Hastings seafront and castle were lit up well beyond midnight. In one of his last duties as Mayor of Hastings, Alderman Rymill sent a loyal message to welcome Queen Elizabeth home, next day attending a thanksgiving service for her safe return.

The official rationing of fats; butter margarine, lard and cooking fats ended on 29th May but the rationing system had already begun to be ignored as far as some shops were concerned. Henceforth, the nation's diet became increasingly high in fat; the amount of food choice in the 1950s was considerably lower than today. Fresh fruit and vegetables were bought mainly from British growers, so people ate what was in season. Strawberries would be in the shops for just a few weeks in the summer and there were no fresh peas, beans or salad in the winter. In the 1950s food was a major part of most families' spending, taking up about a third of the average income. School dinners provided a hot meal at midday for just over half of all children. As during the war, the school meals service continued catering for children from all backgrounds and not just those from poor families. The service was regarded as a great success, producing healthier children and encouraging better behaviour, particularly when children and teachers

1954

The demolition of the Elite Cinema

Marine Court contrasts starkly with James Burton Terrace

1954

The Albert Memorial some time in the early 1950s

Hastings Beach on a Bank Holiday Monday in the 1950s

ate together in small groups. The food was typical 1950s fare; meat and two vegetables, macaroni cheese, fish on Fridays and a dessert such as rice pudding, semolina, tapioca or jam sponge and custard; to today's palate the food of the period would seem bland and monotonous. But a change from this wholesome, stodgy fare was afoot; the books of Elizabeth David were teaching home cooks the sophistications of foreign cuisine. Mrs David spent the war years in France, Greece and Egypt and was horrified on her return to Britain to discover what rationing and shortages had done to the national diet. Her writing introduced the Mediterranean love of food to the British; slowly changing what people ate at home. Shopping also began to be transformed when the bigger food retailers started to open self-service shops, an idea copied from America.

People's expectations of every aspect of their lives were changing; those who had thought it their lot to remain as tenants were becoming home owners. Pre-war built houses were popular purchases; newly-built, post-war houses were smaller than those of pre-war design. Housewives yearned for a fitted kitchen, full of appliances and the modern furniture made by Gomme, notably the G-Plan range, light enough for the housewife to move about unaided and produced in a series of coordinating units that could be bought separately, to meet individual needs. The most common complaint about the G-Plan furniture was that its splayed leg design constantly tripped up the unwary. Women's clothing and dress sense improved remarkably in the 1950s: The higher standard of manufacture of utility clothes had ended the shoddiness of pre-war, mass produced clothing and new skills enabled manufacturers and chain stores to offer quality goods. Any stigma attached to early, ready-made clothes was forgotten, once it was known even royalty bought "off the peg." Marks & Spencer produced the best ready-to-wear chain store clothes; not the cheapest but the best value for money. The fashionable age of being between thirty and forty at the start of the 1950s began to change. Previously, 18-year old girls often dressed and made themselves up to look as old as their mothers; in the mid-1950s teenagers were emerging not merely as a new fashion market but consumers in their own right.

1954

This account of austerity Hastings ends with midnight on 4th July 1954, the hour that brought an end to meat and bacon rationing, the last foods to be freed from a system which had dominated British appetites for 14 years. The Chairman of the Hastings Food Committee received a letter from the Minister of Food, Gwilym Lloyd George, offering warm appreciation for his years of invaluable service. Members of the London Housewives' Association held a special ceremony in London's Trafalgar Square to mark de-rationing day. The Minister of Fuel and Power, Geoffrey Lloyd, burned a large replica of a ration book at an open meeting in his constituency. But the Minister of Food said he would keep his ration book as a souvenir and praised all those traders and organisations that had co-operated with the rationing system. For the first time since the war began London's Smithfield Market opened at midnight instead of 6am and meat sellers were doing a roaring trade. Butcher Alderman Rymill, released on 29th May from his mayoral duties, presided with pleasure behind the counter of his shop in Kings Road.

"Vigilant", Frederick William Goodsell, our commentator through the years in which the tide of austerity slowly turned in Hastings, retired from his position as editor of the Hastings and St Leonards Observer early in 1965, due to a nervous breakdown. He died in April 1972, at the age of 63. These words are from his obituary:

Frederick Goodsell sought to support any move which gave promise of real progress to Hastings and St Leonards through realistic schemes. As a devoted Hastinger he was proud of the town's long history and in particular of its architectural heritage. He also had an appreciation of its role as a seaside resort; he relished the concert parties, the theatre and the long standing musical connections. His musical appreciation stemmed from his appearance in the Hastings Musical Festival as a young pianist. He admired and supported the pre-war Hastings Municipal Orchestra at the White Rock Pavilion and subsequently the London Philharmonic. He was a weekend painter and delighted in the town's links with the world of art and its outstanding School of Art. He was a keen supporter of various charities. It was believed by many that under Goodsell's wartime editorship the Observer helped to sustain the townspeople's morale. He accepted that Hastings was in part changing its role and had to accept industry as a necessary new force to revitalise its economy. But he was conservative enough (with a small c) to hope that much of the true charm of the town could be preserved. These views were reflected in his articles, which were at once lucid and vigorous. He never shirked important issues and accepted philosophically that at times he was crying in the wilderness.

From reading the opinion pieces of Frederick Goodsell and studying the newspaper as a whole one could imagine that he wrote the entire publication; his formal prose style and attitudes permeate every page. Without doubt he set the tone of the Observer in his years as editor. The local paper was held in considerable regard and its critics, if not silent were reasonably respectful. In these less deferential days the local paper is seen as a valid target for the harsh criticisms and complaints it receives and yet for 21,000 Hastings residents and their families reading the Observer is a weekly ritual. Statistics show that 40.5 million people nationwide read a 'local rag.'

Peter Lindsey, aged 39, became Group Editor of today's Hastings and St Leonards Observer in 2005, after ten years with The Eastbourne Herald. Mr Lindsey is accessible and communicative and it was no surprise to learn that he is not one of those editors who sit at their desk all day; he prefers to get out into the community for both professional and social reasons and inevitably, local news stories and topical issues come his way. In response to questions about the style of the present day Observer Mr Lindsey said that he exerts no influence and writes only the front page and his comment column "My Word." The week's stories are selected by the news team, the news editor and the sub-editor, at weekly meetings. He added that his judgement and experience is called upon to assess the validity of some stories and he has to approve every page of each edition.

The progress of the present day Hastings and St Leonards Observer reflects the times; it has a website that is updated several times a day with local news items, photo galleries, video film and a busy public discussion forum. During the years of Frederick Goodsell's editorship the Observer promoted endless good causes; encouraging donations to campaigns that collected millions of pounds for the war effort and supported the work of local charities and societies. The Observer continues that tradition under Peter Lindsey. The most high profile campaign the Observer has run in recent years had been a fight to save the maternity services at Hastings Conquest Hospital. An innovation of which Mr Lindsey is particularly proud is bringing to Hastings a scheme he established in Eastbourne – The Achievers Award; the presentation of the Hastings Achiever's Awards is in October, during the Hastings Week celebrations. The award recognises some of the many people who do so much good for the town and raises money for charity; £20,000 to date. The 2007 event recognised 25 winners, including a surprise Spirit of Hastings award for Kevin Boorman, for all the work he does above and beyond his duties as Hastings Marketing Manager.

Peter Lindsey is often taken to task about Observer front page headlines that reflect the less happy side of Hastings life. He has to remind the public that selling newspapers is a business and good news does not sell. Even Goodsell accepted that fact; headlining anything sensational, albeit in the more restrained manner of his day. The Observer's 2008 post-May Bank Holiday front page, "WE'RE TOPS FOR TRIPPERS' gave rise to some jokes against Peter Lindsey, as he was away when the cheerful headline was prepared. Frederick Goodsell would have been horrified at the headline; his animosity to day trippers is documented. He would have considered a town packed with day visitors a cause for despair, not jubilation.

The last words here must be of Goodsell; Mr. W H Dyer, Hastings Borough Publicity Officer and nephew of Sir Alfred Dyer, wrote the following tribute to his friend.

Freddie was a man of culture who could make written words live ... His leading articles were often referred to in the town as brilliant... Even in later years, when illness had left its mark on him he never lost his grasp of current affairs or his capacity for gentle raillery. He was deeply religious ... I hope that now he has found the peace which his disturbed state of mind denied him here.

In 1945 the Observer published a book that Frederick Goodsell compiled. Called "Hastings and St Leonards in the Front Line" it is a collection of photographs and reports from the wartime editions of the

Observer. The book has become a sought-after and valuable resource to local WWII researchers and writers and a legacy to the town Goodsell cherished.

Part II

Post War
Citizens

The following are the people who have generously contributed details of their post-war, day-to-day lives; providing living witness to Britain's recovery from conflict and its austerity years.

They are today's grandparents and great-grandparents, whose early years and young adulthood were shaped by war and its aftermath.

Moira, aged 14, winner of two Hastings bathing beauty contests in 1948

Moira Hornsey

In April 1947 the White Rock Swimming Baths held an Easter Gala at which a beauty queen was chosen. The Observer reported:

As strains of the songs 'The Volga Boatman' and 'Cruising Down the River' issued from a crowded gallery, a gaily decorated boat floated on the pool with a charming crew of four bathing belles. There were sixteen entrants to the contest and the winner was 17-year-old Moira Knight, who said it was the first time she had entered a beauty competition.

Moira says of her appearance in the bathing beauty contest:

I did not think I would win as I was given the competitor number 13 but from now on it will be my lucky number!

What the competition judges did not know was that Moira was only 14; had they been aware of that she would have been disqualified. Moira's mother had been killed in a motor cycle accident in November 1946 and the 14-year-old had been looking after her father, younger sister and the home ever since.

The following Whitsun she entered and won a beauty contest to celebrate that season's reopening of the St Leonards outdoor bathing pool. Moira was unaware that winning the beauty contest would lead to international recognition. She was photographed wearing the clinging, shirred-elastic bathing suit of the times and smiling happily, posed against the backdrop of the pool. This picture appeared in many overseas publications including those in Australia, South Africa, Hong Kong, America, Ceylon and Norway. Subsequently, Moira not only received fan mail but food parcels too, often vaguely addressed but the postman father of Moira's childhood sweetheart was able to identify the recipient. That summer Moira's father took his daughters on a sombre pilgrimage by motor-cycle and sidecar to visit the places where he had fought during WWII before being stranded on the beaches at Dunkirk. In April 1948 Moira Knight made an official appearance at the Hastings fund-raising exhibition of Goering's Mercedes. She remembers:

The car was horrible and ugly, it seemed weird and ominous. It came to my mind again when I saw the film Schindler's List.

Moira, who worked at Alston's Corsetry shop, was married in June 1952 at the now demolished St Andrews Church, holding the reception in the Baldslow Road house and garden of her sister-in-law. The newlyweds had a flat in a large house nearby; they had a son in 1962. In April 1953 it was announced in the Daily Sketch that Hastings Councillor Major Sims-Hilditch was setting a challenge, "A new Battle of Hastings", and "A publicity stunt", as the paper described it. The article began with the councillor ungallantly disparaging girls from other regions and continued:

I make a challenge to any other city, town or village to produce not one but six local girls who can beat half a dozen from Hastings for their beauty, intelligence and ability to speak the Queen's English. I do not mean beauty queens who win contests.

The photo accompanying the article was a demurely dressed Moira, now Mrs Hornsey, the 1947 Hastings beauty contest winner.

Moira's public appearances continued after marriage: She was an attendant to the Hastings Carnival Queen in 1953, the year in which Vigilant complained of the procession having "Too many queens" but no doubt the crowd lining the route had no objection to the passing spectacle of lots of pretty girls. Moira was given a prize in an Easter-time fashion contest on Hastings Pier and was a model for Mastins, one of Hastings' leading department and fashion stores.

In those days cheerful holiday-related news items about Hastings were featured quite frequently in the national press; Moira, by now manageress of the Debenham's, (formerly Plummer Roddis) corsetry department, became "Iris", the Hastings Daily Express Holiday Girl. During the season the Daily Express used to publish a prize-winning question which readers could answer by speaking to "Iris" who toured

Hastings seafront in her lunch hour, wearing a Daily Express shoulder sash and in so doing, acting as ambassador for her home town.

In 1978 Moira trained as a relief pub manager, taking over the Greyhound Inn at Brighton in 1979; the pub and the surrounding Brighton Lanes were featured in the then newly-released film "Quadrophenia." Moira says:

Fans of the film would make pilgrimages to the inn on bank holidays; they were mostly mods and rockers and so of course there were fights. I found myself taking on the role of a bouncer and I got quite good at knowing when it was the right time to send for the police.

Moira later suffered several bouts of poor health and retired to Hastings. She now lives in a memento-filled, St Leonards Seafront flat, mid-way between the sites of the two swimming pools that were the scenes of her early triumphs. During her personal life and varied career Moira has made and retained a wide circle of friends. She meets bi-monthly with some of these for a "knitting and nattering" group at the King's Head in Battle. As they chat they knit bonnets for African premature babies.

Phyllis and Ron July 1951

Phyllis and Ron Burkin (Victoria Seymour's Family)

Ron Burkin, my brother, was conscripted into the RAF in December 1945 under the Duration of Present Emergencies Regulations. Unlike National Servicemen he was given no demob number and served a total of three years. His entry into the services had been delayed as the result of severe illness during his teens and it was thought that he would not be accepted into the RAF because of his previous bad health; as it was he passed Al. Ron was keen to join up as he believed that it was past time for him to cut the apron strings and to see life. He was still weak from the years of illness and he found the gruelling initial training very hard going but he said that it aided his full recovery.

Ron was demobbed in 1948 but did not return immediately to Hastings, as the employment situation in the town was not good. However, in 1949 circumstances obliged him to join our family home on a farm at Fairlight, where our parents were employed. The job situation in Hastings was still poor so Ron took casual farm work and for two seasons he was a temporary postal worker in the sorting office at Christmas. There he met an older man from the Hastings fishing community who offered him work at sea. Our dad was hotly opposed to this idea as he knew having her son in hazardous work would worry our mother, so he threatened to throw Ron out of the house if he became a fisherman.

In 1950 Ron, by then engaged to Phyllis, found a job with Briggs Motors at Dagenham, making car bodies for Fords. He left home and got a flat near his work. Ron and Phyllis married in 1951. They chose to have a modest, registry office wedding; their opinion being that an ostentatious wedding was not what their marriage was about. Phyllis wore a dark green suit with brown accessories and a corsage of pale green, brown-spotted orchids, which were a luxury then and had to be specially ordered. Phyllis thought the suit would do service after the wedding; at that time most well-dressed women reckoned to own a tailored suit. Victoria says of the wedding party's attire:

"My mother made herself a navy dress for the wedding and one in pale blue for me; she crocheted our "regulation" white lace gloves. Then, as now, the hat was an expensive addition to the ensemble. So to meet this need my mother went back to her hard-up Victorian childhood. My grandmother had taught her to make smart-looking hats from crepe paper. Paper of the desired colour was cut into bands across the grain and these were plaited to make a long strip. This was formed into the hat's crown and a brim in the chosen style, deep or shallow, was added from further paper plaits. I thought that the end result, decorated with a spray of artificial flowers and a wisp of veiling looked rather smart. We just hoped it did not rain; it proved to be a dry, swelteringly hot day."

The reception was held at the bride's family home; photos were taken in the garden against a background of pink rambling roses. After one night alone in Ron's parental home at Fairlight; the couple then travelled by bus to their Isle of Wight honeymoon. They returned to the rented accommodation that Ron had been living in for some time; there was no chance of their being put on a council housing list as neither of them met the residency criteria. Phyllis said,

I had no kitchen so did my cooking in our rooms, on one gas ring, much of it in the newly popular Prestige pressure cooker. On Sundays I was permitted by the landlady to use her oven to cook a roast but the washing up had to be done in our sitting room in a bowl on an enamel topped table. I also did the laundry there, in a tin bath. I borrowed the landlady's wringer and then hung the washing on an outdoor line but if it was wet I put it on a clothes horse to dry in our rooms.

After six months Phyllis got a job as an armature winder, which helped with the family income, leaving work to have her first child. Ron set about teaching himself DIY carpentry, with his only previous experience being school woodwork classes and the backyard construction of go-carts and sledges. Ron says,

My first effort was a double sink unit. We had paid a deposit on a custom made model but I was put on short time at work and we could

not pay the balance; the shop refused to return the deposit. I bought a double metal drainer and then the wood, bit by bit. With a few very basic tools I eventually completed the job, saving two thirds of the price of the shop model and to a standard that would have made my old woodwork teacher proud. It seemed to impress the plumber, whose skills I had not attained at that time, when he came to connect the unit to the water supply.

Phyllis and Ron both worked hard, economized and saved and by 1954 they were able to buy their first house. They have three children including twin boys, and six grandchildren.

Joyce Brewer on Hastings Pier in the 1950's

Joyce Brewer

Joyce Brewer, a milk delivery girl, remembers the huge piles of rubble that accumulated around the town post-war, as demolition gangs pulled down bombed houses damaged beyond repair. She says:

The wood was put in separate piles and people were invited to help themselves. I took away a lot of wood in my milk van, for my family and others. We did not get much for free then and I wasn't going to miss this chance. In 1946 there was a highlight in my life. I'd heard that a Miss Kite over at Harley Shute, just a country lane then, was giving riding lessons so I cycled over to see her; she charged 3/6d (seventeen and a half pence) per hour for riding instruction. Cigarettes were hard to come by then so I paid Miss Kite, a smoker, with a packet of twenty, which cost the same as the riding lesson. I booked up to take an hour's lesson per week, after I had finished my milk round. We took gentle trots round the lanes and streets of St Leonards. For the following six days my legs were stiff and painful and by the time I had recovered another riding lesson was due. After a few months I realised horse-riding was not the pastime for me. I was already worn out delivering milk up and down Hastings' thousands of steps.

Joyce celebrated her 21st birthday on 26th February 1947, one of the worst winters in living memory. Joyce recalls:

Friends struggled to my party down an unmade road that had become like a skating rink. My mum gave up her sugar ration so that my birthday cake could have an icing-sugar coating. It was a very austere party but we enjoyed ourselves.

At work conditions were Arctic; the milk was frozen solid in the bottles and Joyce developed chilblains on her back-side from sitting on the van's cold leather seat. When the snow made it impossible to drive Joyce transported the milk in crates fixed on a sledge, never missing a customer.

There were changes to Joyce's home life. Her two sisters married soldiers and moved away from the area; Joyce remained at home with her parents and brother. She felt the need for some female company and a change from the tough outdoor job she had done for eight years. In the spring of 1949 Joyce took a job in a small factory in Parker Road; it was one of the few sources of light industrial work in the town at that time. Joyce got a lower wage than for the milk round for what proved to be very boring work. She says:

My job was using a machine to cover very fine wire with silk thread by machines; these were very old and did not work well. I was constantly in hot water with the supervisor. The wages were only two to three pounds a week with a 2/6 (twelve and a half pence) bonus if we produced enough reels of wire. It was a big drop from my milk round wage of four pounds per week, with generous tips at Christmas, which totalled £20 at 1948.

But the wage at the factory was not as important as the fact that Joyce soon made new friends:

I experimented with make up and new clothes and we went to the cinema, dancing, roller-skating, speedway, table tennis and swimming. We met up with a gang of nice chaps and together we went to a couple of London shows and on holiday to the Isle Wight and Butlin's Holiday Camp at Clacton; it cost about seven pounds a week. All food and entertainments were included in the price so only a little extra spending money was needed.

The meals were taken in a vast restaurant that seated about 1000 and Joyce's recollection of the cuisine was that there seemed to be a lot of sausages and beans. Everything was much regimented and Joyce said that the male holiday makers did not like the system as it was too much like the armed services of their recent memory. It did however give a complete break for the mothers; the after-dark "baby-sitting" chalet patrols and the on-site entertainments for children created a secure environment – a thing precious to the war-raised generation. Although holiday camps became a byword for highly organised activities and cheesy entertainment many people look back on them fondly.

Joyce and her pals were very fond of walking:

We would take our dogs and ramble all over the countryside, day and night. In the afternoons we would go down town to walk the seafront to St Leonards and have coffee then queue up at the Gaiety or Ritz cinemas and walk home by 11pm.

Joyce visited the Festival of Britain with a coach party; her favourite part of the exhibition was the Dome of Discovery. She was impressed by a display of a new method of manufacturing tyres. She said that the dome also had a mock- up of what would happen if the ice caps melted, putting London 90 feet below water; a fantasy in 1951. As austerity lifted it became possible for girls to buy nice things; Joyce remembers a pair of shoes she brought from Kay's catalogue, paying for them by weekly instalments. She said they were green suede, flat-heeled with green suede tassels on the laces. She also spoke about a pair of stockings she got from Plummer Roddis in Hastings; they were Bear Brand, pure silk and cost an enormous 17/6d (seventy-seven pence). Silk and nylon stockings were hand-repaired at Plummers up until the mid-1950s. The repairer sat in public view, with the stocking stretched over a frame, under an illuminated magnifying glass. It was a tedious and sometimes smelly job, as not all the stockings were properly washed before being handed in! Joyce continued;

Eventually the work slackened off at the factory and some of us, including me, were stood off. Apart from seasonal work there was not a lot on offer in the way of employment so in 1954 a friend and I took ourselves off to Luton, where we heard that jobs were plentiful, especially in the car trade. My friend Joan went to the Skafco ball-bearing factory and I went to Commer Cars. We both lodged with my Aunt Hilda whose husband had died in a Japanese prisoner of war camp. My work at Commer Cars was operating a drill about eight feet high, with which I made holes in various sized car parts. The wages and bonuses were very good for the time - about eight pounds per week. I lived well and bought many records of popular singers of the day – Dean Martin, Guy Mitchell, Frankie Laine. The workers at Commer were mainly men, so much for female company at work. They were nice chaps and always helpful, but not above wolf-whistling my friend and I, as we walked through the gangways. Not that we were fashionably dressed; for safety we wore steel-toe-capped boots, navy-blue overalls, a cap with peak at the front and a net at the back, to stop our hair from catching in the drill. As we worked a white fluid ran over the drill to keep it cool. This fluid played havoc with our hands; it was unsafe to wear gloves doing this work. There were sharp coils of waste metal, called swarf, which flew off the machine. They were far from comfortable working conditions; the glass roof above my machine leaked during wet weather and when I complained to the forelady she said that when the weather was dry the leak could not be located and when it was wet it was too dangerous to look for it. Her solution was to give me a piece of sacking to put over my shoulders.

In spite of everything I liked Luton and working at Commer and I had some good times with friends, going home for a family visit every third week. I was worried about my Dad's health and wondered if I should go home permanently but my mum discouraged this idea. But a telegram sent me hurrying home, arriving the day before my dad died. It was time for me to look after mum. I took a succession of jobs in Hastings that did not pay well. Then a vacancy occurred for work as a railway carriage cleaner at Ore Station, very close to my home. If I had the idea that this was an easy job I was soon proved wrong. I worked with a gang of women: As the trains came into the sheds we had to jump aboard and clean carriages from end to end with a mop, brushes and a flannel, empty the ashtrays and polish every window before the train moved out for journeys to London or Brighton. We also had to clean the high carriage ceilings every so often, a difficult job as we were forbidden to get water on the seat cushions. The job I hated most was vacuuming the seats. We plugged a heavy pipe into various points in the shed floor then dragged this pipe into each carriage, about five feet above the ground and ran the nozzle over every inch of the velvet-covered seats. It was a dusty and back-breaking job and very hot work on summer days. I stuck it for two years then suffered a slipped disc and was obliged to pack it in. The money may have been better than the factory but it was not work I would recommend. I suffered repeated sessions on the 'rack' (traction) at the Royal East Sussex Hospital and six months off work before I recovered.

I then found a position as a driver and stores manager at £8 a week and stayed in it for 15 years, until 1962. After this I did stores work and driving for our local Fiat garage. I took early retirement in 1985 as my mother became too ill to be left on her own; she died a year later, aged 84. I have often wondered how differently my life would have turned out if there had never been a war. I would most likely have finished my education at Hastings High School for Girls and gone on to college to train for a decent career. But as it was I ended up in a series of unskilled jobs but at least I learned to drive free of charge. My years of heavy, outdoor work in all weathers built a strong constitution and meeting so many people gave me, formerly a shy person, the confidence to tackle life. As for marriage, I only ever fancied one or two chaps, who fate had destined for other partners. Maybe I wasn't meant to marry.

Kathleen and Ron Upton, September 1946

Kathleen and Ron Upton

Kathleen Upton was born in Northiam and moved to Hastings in 1934. She met her husband-to-be Ron when they were both 12; he was the newspaper delivery boy who politely held open the front garden gate of her home so she could pass through. Ron was called up aged 18 to work as a Bevin Boy: There was a severe shortage of miners so some service conscripts, selected randomly by the final numbers in their registration code, were obliged to work in the coal mines instead of going into the services. When Ron and the other Bevin Boys started to compare notes it seemed that their selection had not been quite as random as they had been led to believe. In fact, "It looked like a fiddle," as Ron put it. Most of the Bevin Boys had no background in mining and hated the job, feeling that being drafted down the pit was stigmatised as being the place where conscientious objectors were sent. After 16 months in the mines Ron applied to join the army and probably because of his height and build, he was put in the military police.

Kathleen's family moved to 27 Lewis Road, Hollington on 1st January 1939. Behind the house were allotments, where the tower blocks now stand. In a nearby lane there was a house called "The Choice", in which lived a 70-year old man called John Whatman. He worked the surrounding land as a smallholding, rearing pigs and dealing in horses. One snowy Saturday night in March 1946 a John Smith, who lived with the gypsies at Little Common, went to rob Whatman and in the course the robbery the farmer was shot dead; the murderer left his footprints in the snow. Ex-Inspector Banks said of the case, "It was known that Whatman had a large sum of money and this was found when his house was being cleared; it was stuffed in a paraffin heater. Smith was arrested in a public house in Markyate, Hertfordshire when he was trying to sell a gold watch and two rings he had stolen from Whatman. He was caught because he could not read and the watch was engraved with John Whatman's name. Smith was hung at Pentonville prison."

When Hastings beach re-opened towards the end of the war, Kathleen's parents took up their pre-war custom of hiring, for twelve shillings (60p) per year, a beach tent that the attendants chained to the sea wall at night. Kathleen said, "We just lived on the beach all summer, swimming and having picnics." She worked as a florist at the Silverhill greengrocery store owned by the Bailey family. Kathleen was trained by Doris Bailey to make bouquets and wreaths, sadly in urgent demand after bombing raids.

Kathleen and Ron married at Upper Park Road Methodist Church, Bohemia, in September 1946. Kathleen said that her dress, in off-white satin with a nightdress as petticoat, was borrowed, as were the very high-heeled shoes, which were extremely uncomfortable; she was the fourth bride to wear the dress. The senior bridesmaid was a friend, who wore a borrowed blue dress; the two younger bridesmaids were twins, wearing salmon pink taffeta dresses, made by their mother, a neighbour. Kathleen was told that when she was a child she had seen the new-born twins in their cot and said, "I am glad they are girls; they will be my bridesmaids one day." Kathleen said that post-war it was difficult to get hot-house flowers as no fuel was permitted for greenhouses but as her wedding was in September there were plenty of flowers available. Kathleen carried red carnations; the bridesmaid in blue had pink carnations and the twins' bouquets were blue scabious and white gypsophillia. The reception was held at Ferrari's Restaurant, situated where The Logie Baird pub now stands. During the worst of the austerity period wedding receptions were limited to 50 guests, a regulation likely to cause discord in the most harmonious of families. As well as food rationing the recently imposed bread rationing was in force so the menu was necessarily simple: ham salad, fruit salad and wedding cake; this was made at The Creamery, a high-class bakery shop and tea rooms in Robertson Street.

Kathleen and Ron honeymooned in London, spending the week like tourists, seeing all the famous sites as well as paying a visit to the "Britain Can Make It Exhibition." On their return to Hastings Ron went back to barracks and Kathleen to live with her family. When Ron came out of the army in 1948 the couple lived in a large front bedroom in Kathleen's home; a year later they found a one-bedroomed garden flat. Vivienne, their daughter was born in 1950 in St Helen's Hospital.

Kathleen recalls,

The maternity ward was pretty basic in those days, as far as facilities were concerned. There were no curtains round the beds and if you had to have an enema or examination the staff wheeled along low screens made from thin fabric. Often the nurses asked us to express our surplus breast milk for the premature babies. We were given two mugs each and left to get on with it. One day there we were, fourteen new mothers busy with our mugs and in full view, when the vicar and his acolytes hurried through the ward, on the way to an urgent call. It was red faces all round!

In 1953 Kathleen and Ron decided to emigrate to Australia. In 1992 Kathleen published a book about her experiences, "To the Undiscovered Ends." From the book's first paragraphs it's clear that not everyone felt that the coronation marked a favourable turn in the tide of their prospects. Kathleen wrote:

It was Coronation Week, bleak, wet and utterly miserable. More like November than June and we felt as miserable as the weather....We were living in a damp flat with no bathroom; we were low on the council housing list because we were termed as being adequately housed. We were unable to find anywhere else to live and we had no money for a deposit on a house, even if one had been available.

Kathleen's husband was working as a fireman on the railway when steam engines were being phased out in favour of diesels. He was based at Reading, mostly working late shifts. Unable to get transport home he slept for a few hours in a railway carriage until he could get an early train. The couple had just a few hours together and then Ron would have to be off again until the next morning. Their little daughter had severe asthma and her parents were advised by the hospital specialist that a couple of years in a warmer climate would improve her condition. A chance remark by Ron, "What about Australia?", altered the course of their lives. The couple began a seemingly endless paper chase to find a sponsor and to be granted the subsidised travel costs; becoming what the Australians called "Ten Pound Poms."

They left England in 1954; although seasick for most of the time Kathleen wrote warmly of the wonderful sights, friendships and her experiences during the family's voyage to Australia. After the comfort on board ship the bleak reception and type of accommodation they encountered on arriving in Australia were an appalling contrast. Their many problems were increased by Lloyds Bank in England failing to transfer to Australia the £250 they had saved to see them through the first few months. They were dismayed to discover that some indigenous Australians were hostile to "Pommie bastards" and that many disenchanted emigrants from Great Britain were saving to pay for their passage back home.

Kathleen said that support for new immigrants in Australia in the early 1950s was almost non-existent and that the true facts about the hard conditions they faced were not made clear to applicants for the assisted passage scheme. Judging from her book, Kathleen was not a "whingeing Pom;" in fact her courage, resourcefulness, sense of humour and above all, the support of a good husband carried her through, until their return to Great Britain in 1956. In February 2008 Kathleen appeared in the BBC TV history series Timewatch, in an episode called "The Ten Pound Poms." Ron died nearly four years ago and Kathleen now lives in a cosy flat not far from where in her childhood she roamed the fields of Hollington.

George Miller

During the early part of the war George Miller was apprenticed as a mechanical engineer at Battersea Power Station, in London. He joined the Royal Engineers and was parachuted into Arnhem in 1944. George was demobilised in 1948 and completed the final two years of his apprenticeship at the power station. He lived in Queen's Road, which was adjacent to Battersea Park and he witnessed the construction of the Festival of Britain attractions; workmen on the site lodged in his family home. Aged 21 George married Beryl and they decided they would prefer to raise their family away from London.

In 1951 Beryl went to the railway station and got on the first train that was leaving, which by chance was going to Hastings. She looked at properties in the town and later she and George bought a semi-detached house in Amherst Road. The estate agent who sold them the house told George that there was plenty of work in the area saying, "You could get a job tomorrow." George intended to work at Hastings Broomgrove Power Station but he learned that it only operated in the winter, when there was extra demand. So to pay their £2,000 mortgage George took a grindingly hard job at the gypsum mines at Robertsbridge, 12 miles from Hastings, cycling both ways. The Millers soon sold the Amherst Road house for a profit and bought 34 Cambridge Gardens; the property was somewhat dilapidated but they did it up and ran it as a guest house, called St Anthony's. George said that in 1951 Hastings was still looking very run down and depressed. On the lighter side he remembered seeing the Guinness Clock at the Old Town during its Festival of Britain visit and thinking it was a clever piece of mechanical engineering.

George got a job in maintenance at the bottling plant of the brewery company, Watney Combe Reid, in Hastings Old Town; he also took on extra work as a sales rep for the firm and was soon in a position of responsibility. George says:

Six or seven years after arriving in Hastings the estate agent who had supplied misleading information to me about the employment situation in Hastings, applied to the brewers for a job; it was I who interviewed him; you can guess the outcome.

The Millers decided to put the guest house on the market. A rough-looking prospective buyer, a barrow boy from London, liked the look of St Anthony's and asked if he could stay the weekend; his hosts were a bit concerned, fearing he was a trickster but they let him stay. When they asked him in the morning if he understood the asking price for the property he said, "Yes I do and I have got the cash with me, it's upstairs, in a shoe box under the bed!"

The Millers eventually moved to a house called "Sunnyside" in Greystone Lane, behind Christ Church in Ore Village. George remembers:

In the mid-1950s Ore was a thriving business community, with four butchers, two greengrocers, three grocers, a fishmonger, two shoe shops, two ironmongers, a seed and corn merchant, a drapery shop, a post office, newsagent, bakers and confectioners, a watchmaker and a chemist. There were two banks, a doctor, solicitor and a lending library. "Sunnyside" had a good bit of ground at the back and we kept goats; one billy goat was an expert escapologist and on a jaunt he found his way to Cornelius the greengrocer, where he ate a whole tray of peaches.

Over a period of many years the Millers acquired various properties in Hastings and St Leonards, including the Inver Gordon Hotel in Warrior Square. Now a widower, George has become a significant figure in local property and business circles; he has been a member of the prestigious Winkle Club since 1970 and is Chairman of the Seafront Traders Association. George's one time neighbour was Sidney Little, the Hastings revolutionary borough engineer. George regarded him as:

Brilliant in his planning, a man before his times and very clever. In appearance he was smart, even dapper. He always called me George and I called him Mr Little.

To mark the 50th anniversary of the D-Day landings in May 1994, 75-

George Miller with Prince Charles at the 1994 D-Day 50th anniversary

year old George and 29 other ex-paratroopers made a jump over Arnhem. They had to pass a medical and then make six practice jumps. The veterans spent the night before the commemorative jump together in barracks. One of their number had a wooden leg and his mates hid it. It seems soldiers are never too old for a practical joke. George says:

The jump was made from a Fokker and we had to run towards the back of the plane and leap out of its open hatch, which I found to be a wonderful experience. At Arnhem I was introduced to Princes Charles; the Prince brushed aside my courtesies and said, "It is my *honour to meet* you."

For over 50 years George has watched Hastings struggle to regain status as a coastal resort and he speaks with frustration at what he sees as missed opportunities by the local authority. George has never regretted coming to Hastings; he loves it here and says:

Its people are great. The town is full of opportunities but you have to identify and seize them. If you can't make it in Hastings you can't make it anywhere.

Pam and Ron Garnar

Pam Garnar's story of her post-war life and marriage in her own words:

I was 11 years old when my mother died, maybe an awkward age for my father to deal with. Within two years he had married a woman only 8 years older than me. I did not fit in and was put in a boarding school. This arrangement proved to be too much for my father financially and for reasons I discovered some years after, I was sent to the National Children's Home in Harpenden, Hertfordshire. From that time, until I was 19 years old and needed parental permission to marry, I never heard from my father. When I left the children's home aged fourteen I lodged with a very nice family near London but left them to go into a YMCA hostel, which was nearer my secretarial job in the city, where I worked for a firm of Chartered surveyors. A lot of our work involved visiting many of the old Lipton's and Home and Colonial grocery stores, assessing the war damage and typing up the specifications. I started there in 1946 at a wage of £3.50 a week. It was an interesting job but often miserably cold, dark and wet, as we worked in the damaged warehouses at the back of the shops.

Whilst employed by this firm I made friends with a girl called Audrey and I was invited to spend a weekend at her home. On the Saturday evening we went to a social at the local community hall and after for a coffee in a neighbour's house. There I met Ron; he had been with the GPO since leaving school but had spent five years in India doing military service with the Royal Army Service Corp. Ron asked me and Audrey if we would like to take their dog for a walk but only I accepted and that was when we became friends; 11 months later we were married, on a rather cold dreary March day in 1949. I can remember asking the florist to make my bouquet of lilies which she objected to doing, as to her it was a funeral flower so I ended up with red and white carnations. It was pity, I am tall and I thought that the larger blooms would be more suitable for me. But the florist was a friend of a friend so it was rather difficult to raise objections. I cannot

Pam and Ron Garner March 1949

remember if I hired or borrowed my wedding dress but do not recall having it after the wedding but I kept my veil for some years. Unfortunately no one told me that I had bent my headdress getting out of the car at the church and we only realised what had happened when we saw the photographs. My two bridesmaids were friends, Audrey of course and Joy, a particular friend from the National Children's Home. They wore turquoise dresses and carried bouquets of spring flowers.

My grandmother asked me what we would like for a wedding gift and I wanted a blue eiderdown. She was not too happy about the colour because according to her blue faded so quickly. My father actually turned up with my stepmother for the wedding and gave me away. He presented us with a canteen of cutlery as a wedding gift, some pieces of which I still have nearly 60 years on. I felt badly that Ron's parents paid for the reception; I do not remember my father offering to pay towards it. Most of the guests were my husband's family; he had many cousins with a number of children between them. It was suggested that we invite the parents with their oldest child only and most people were happy with this but one cousin wrote, "Tell your future wife to get off her high horse, unless all our children are invited we won't come." It's strange now to think that I grew closer to that cousin over the years than all the others. The reception was held in a church hall and the catering was adequate in spite of rationing. The only item on the menu I remember now is trifle.

Our honeymoon was spent at the Old Cock Inn, near the children's home I had lived in. I recall that the owner of the inn was a carbon copy of actress Margaret Rutherford, who nearly always played eccentric old ladies. Charles Hill, the Radio Doctor came to the inn a couple of times for dinner. One could not mistake his booming voice. We returned from our honeymoon to set up home with Ron's parents; they let us have the upper floor of their terrace house. I believe they paid less than £500 for the property when it was newly built. We shared the kitchen and bathroom but it worked out well and I got on with my parents-in-law very happily. My father-in-law had lost an arm in the First World War; I remember him saying how much his phantom little finger hurt. He worked for Standard Telephone and Cables as a commissionaire, a post that often went to wounded ex-service men at the time.

We lived with my husband's parents until 1955 when I had my first son, with another arriving in 1957. We then bought a house owned by Ron's aunt, who moved in with his mother; she was a widow by then. We stayed in that house until our sons had grown up. Two months before our eldest son married we decided to move to St Leonards. My husband commuted to London until his retirement from the job that he had held all his life, apart from his war service. I lost him to the wretched Motor Neurone disease in 1989, a few weeks after celebrating our Ruby Wedding Anniversary.

Hilda and Jim Barker

Hilda Brewer met Jim Barker during the war; he was one of the soldiers who manned the ack-ack guns defending the railway and power stations, near Hilda's home in Hastings. Hilda and Jim were married at Hastings Registry Office on 18th August 1944. As with so many weddings in wartime, it was a modest affair. Hilda's father and her sister Joyce could not get time off work to attend the ceremony so only her mother, other sister Barbara and future brother-in-law were present. With no wedding reception the newly-married couple set off immediately by train for a brief honeymoon at Jim's home in Manchester where they would live with his mother. The newlyweds stopped on the journey at Brighton Station, where Hilda's father, a train driver, was able to join them for a quick drink. Hilda returned to Hastings in April 1945 to give birth to her first child in St Helen's hospital. Mothers had to pay for the confinement and maternity care; it cost six pounds ten shillings, which Hilda had to find out of her two pounds per week allowance as an army wife. She managed to get the baby's layette together even though everything was still rationed or in short supply; she and her family made the baby's clothes, and customers on her sister's milk round had helped out with a second hand cot and pram. There was a nine-month waiting list in the baby goods shop for these items. Hilda eventually had two sons and now has four grandchildren and five great-grandchildren.

Hilda made clothes for her children and herself for years but didn't let the fact of her being a housewife inhibit her fashion consciousness. She soon gained a reputation among her Manchester neighbours for being smart-looking and her habit of always wearing a hat when she went out brought forth the comment, "Who does he think she is, the district nurse?" Make up was in very short supply during the war but Hilda had never used it to excess, just lipstick and powder, not mascara or eye-shadow; although she admitted to being very fond of nail polish. She mentioned the arrival in the shops of pancake make up; combined foundation and face powder in an easily applied stick.

Hilda and Jim Barker in the 1950s

Food rationing still limited recipes choice; feeling experimental Hilda cooked Jim macaroni cheese for his dinner, which he refused with disgust. In those times macaroni was considered an ingredient for a sweet milk pudding as was rice, unless it accompanied that rare and exotic dish – curry. Because Hilda's father worked for the railway he was able to send her boxes of home grown vegetables, which she shared with neighbours. Family holidays were mostly taken in Hastings; Hilda recalled the only formal holiday she had with her husband and children, in a caravan at Rhyl in 1950. She said, "It was not a holiday park as we know them today but just a caravan in a field but we enjoyed it very much." She said that in those days if you went to a guest house you had to take your ration books along. Hilda said, "In those pre-television years, for the majority, radio and films were the main source of entertainment. It was very common to see long queues snaking round the outside of the buildings when a new film came to town. At the Gaiety Cinema the queue would wind round and round its large foyer, looking like a human Swiss roll."

With James' mother dying soon after her son's marriage and Hilda's family far away they had no baby-sitters so had to take turns to go to pictures. On the radio Hilda enjoyed Tommy Handley's "ITMA", a comedy show that attracted 16 million listeners at the peak of its popularity, as well as 'Two Way Family Favourites'. This was a Sunday lunch-time gramophone record request programme for forces overseas that was presented by a variety of personalities, including Jean Metcalfe, broadcasting from the UK with fellow presenter Cliff Michelmore in a studio in Germany. Previously unknown to each other before their on-air connection they fell in love and married in 1950. No wonder then that Hilda described the programme as, "so romantic!" Big Bill Campbell's Rocky Mountain Rhythms was on Hilda's listening list, even though her husband remarked that Bill came from Salford. Actually a misconception; he came to the UK from North America to fight in WWI and never returned to his home country.

Hilda was a keen reader of Women's magazines, favourites being Woman, Woman's Own and Women's Weekly. Hilda said that she turned first to the knitting patterns but also enjoyed the "letters to the editor" section and the problem pages. She expresses dismay at what she sees as the crude content of many of today's magazines for women.

Now widowed, Hilda still lives in the house she went to as a young bride but she makes a visit to Hastings every year.

Olive and Jack Peddlesden

Olive was born in Hastings in 1922. During the war and after her evacuation from Hastings to Chelmsford she worked in the War Office, in a building that overlooked Buckingham Palace. Olive met her husband Jack at a dance at the White Rock Pavilion in the spring of 1946 and they were engaged by the following August. After his demobilisation Jack returned to his job at Hastings Borough Treasurers; Olive worked at the Police HQ offices, above a gentlemen's outfitters, on the opposite corner to the Gaiety Cinema, now the Odeon. Olive spoke of going to see the Victory Parade in June 1946; she sat in Trafalgar Square all night to keep her place, making occasional forays to Lyon's Corner House for cups of tea. Olive said, "The crowds waiting overnight were happy but noisy so there was no hope of sleep. The Commonwealth troops in the parade were camped out in Hyde Park for several days. I felt proud and emotional on seeing the parade, it was very impressive."

Olive's wedding plans were brought forward by an unexpected housing opportunity. Jack's army pal had been widowed; his young wife had died of tuberculosis and their rented home, fully furnished and equipped, was available. Olive and Jack were married at Christ Church in Ore Village in March 1947. Olive wore, as many brides did in those days, a borrowed dress; it was made of white figured satin. She had three bridesmaids in attendance and Olive sacrificed her own clothing coupons to buy the two older girls new dresses in blue. The third bridesmaid, a child, wore a borrowed dress. Olive's father, a former Great War soldier and a very reclusive man, did not give her away nor did he attend the wedding nor the wedding of her four sisters. Jack's father, a coach driver, arranged for a bus to take the wedding guests from the church to the White Rock Pavilion Restaurant for the reception. After spending one night in the Charing Cross Hotel, Olive and Jack travelled to Exeter, from where they toured the region. Olive said that before marriage she was unable to sew or cook and she took two night classes a week to learn these skills. Olive and Jack had their first child in October 1948 so Olive was able to enjoy the benefits of

Olive & Jack Peddlesden March 1947

the new National Health Service.

Jack got tickets for Olive to go to the London Olympic Games in 1948; she was heavily pregnant and the man sitting next to her asked her not to get too excited in case it precipitated events! Olive saw the Dutch athlete, Fanny Blankers-Koen compete; she was a 30-year-old mother of two and made history at the 1948 Olympics by winning four gold medals. Britain was given only three years to get ready for the games; rationing of food and clothes was still in force, all commodities were in short supply and the rebuilding of bombed homes was held back by lack of materials. There were no new arenas for the London 1948 Olympic Games, existing locations were used; Wembley Stadium, the Empire pool in Wembley and abandoned relics from the 1924 British Empire Exhibition. Neither was there special accommodation for the athletes; most slept under canvas in Richmond Park and were transported to the arena in buses. But the feeling for the Olympic Games was tremendous, as was the interest in all sport at the time; it lifted the country's morale. The games closed in a simple way with all the competitors parading in the stadium, none of the grandiose art-dance-drama display and fireworks which have become part of the Olympic Games in recent decades.

Referring to other events of national importance during the austerity years Olive had no particular memories of these. They occurred at a time when the public were not subjected to a constant onslaught of news, as it is today. Olive said that then, as now, the caring for and rearing of babies and toddlers tended to distract a young a mother's attention from the outside world. However, Olive had an early involvement in the Hastings scheme of twinning with European towns and hers was one of the first families to take up hosting overseas students when all food rationing finally ceased in the summer of 1954. From both ventures she formed friendships that continue to this day.

John Goodall, Founding Principal of Hastings College of Further Education

John Goodall

Before the war John Goodall, father of Helen Bird, who is secretary to Hastings Mayor, was a primary school teacher. He did wartime service with the Royal Air Force and was demobilised in 1946, with the rank of acting wing commander.

John returned to the teaching profession at Clive Vale Junior School but he missed the challenge of leadership that he had enjoyed in the RAF. One afternoon in 1948 John was overseeing a game of football on the East Hill when Hastings Chief Education Officer, Mr Melvyn Outlaw Palmer, appeared and asked if he would like to establish a college of further education in the town. Daughter Helen said, "Of course, it would never happen this way today but these were different times." John Goodall, a chartered engineer, had already been offered a job at Marconi, heading a department; it was the town's good fortune that he decided to remain in Hastings.

The origins of the College of Further Education can be traced to 1891 when the Hastings School of Science was opened on the top floor of 42 George Street, over a printing works. The accommodation consisted of one general laboratory for physics, chemistry and biology and one adjacent classroom. In 1898 the Hastings Evening Continuation Board School for Boys was set up in the St Mary in the Castle School, Portland Place. Two years later a second evening school, for girls, was established in the same premises. The male and female departments were amalgamated in 1912. A new school for learning the building trade, accommodated in premises at Waterloo Place in Hastings, was opened in 1948 with 45 apprentices. This developed, with the addition of five other buildings, into the Hastings Technical Institute.

In the following three years engineering classes were started; five years later the engineering enrolments outstripped those for building. In September 1949 the Hastings Hotel and Catering School was opened at 4-6 West Hill Road, operating full-time courses for 18 students for the catering industry. In 1956 the four separate organisations – technical, science, commercial studies, and hotel and catering were brought under one administrative control with John Goodall as Founder Principal. John appointed his former head at Clive Vale Junior School as head of the Department of General Studies, at the newly established college at Archery Road.

A former colleague of John Goodall is Mr Dudley R Blois; he was a part-time tutor at Hastings Technical Institute, 1957 to 1959 and a full-time lecturer, later a director, at Hastings College of Arts and Technology from 1960 to 2000. Mr Blois says:

John Goodall had a wonderful vision of the technical college for Hastings and St Leonards. He brought together, as previously stated, a very wide range of vocational education institutes, each individual in their own way, embracing engineering, building (construction), science, humanities, art and design, commercial and business studies, hotel and catering. Each department was lead by professionals with teams of highly competent and dedicated lecturers together with many support and administration staff. Mr Goodall had built the college, providing excellent resources for all students and meeting the needs of local employers, of which the town and locality were very proud. He was an inspirational principal who laid down firm foundations which allowed the college (Hastings College of Arts and Technology) to go on to national and international recognition in later years.

Helen Bird says of her father:

He was a warm and welcoming man, a good captain of his ship; he knew his staff and their families well and created a relaxed atmosphere in the college, with students being treated as young adults.

When Helen had the choice on leaving school of either working in Hall's, the shoe shop, or taking a commercial course at the college, she chose the latter. She says,

Although my father was the principal of the college it did not make any difficulties for us. Most of the time we did not speak but if we were obliged to do so I called him Mr Goodall. Only the staff knew that I was his daughter.

John Goodall retired in August 1977. He and his wife Joyce were given a retirement dinner by the college's Hotel and Catering Advisory Committee. The breadth of John's commitment to Hastings may be judged by the list of organisations to which he gave his time, during both his working and retirement years. He was a member of the British Productivity Association, The Federation of Sussex Industries, The Hotel and Catering Industrial Training Board Advisory Council, The Civil Services Council, The Southern Philharmonic Association, The Stables Trust, Cancer Relief, and The Wild Bird Preservation Trust.

Joan and Bill Henry

Joan was born in Poplar in the East End of London. She joined the ATS Pay Corp in 1942 and married Bill, who was in the RAF in 1944. War was being waged on the home front and everything was in short supply but the bridal photograph suggests peace and plenty. Joan told me that almost everything for the wedding was borrowed; her dress, the bridegroom's black jacket and striped trousers and the bridesmaids' assorted sweet pea shade dresses; only their pastel feather headdresses were new. The bride had spent the night before her wedding in the family's Anderson Shelter, (just visible in the background of the photo) when an air raid kept everyone awake. The threat of further raids made the official photographer afraid to turn up at the church; hence the photos were taken later, in the garden, with the wedding party trying not to tread on the cabbages. The reception was at Joan's home. Her mother made a two-tier wedding cake, almost unheard of at the time. Her husband suggested it must have been made with black market dried fruit. The meal was ham and salad; some guests contributed food; Joan's auntie, visiting from Thurnham near Maidstone, brought fresh strawberries. The newly weds were not able to have a honeymoon but later they shared a spell of leave, when they went to the Isle of Wight, off limits to all but service personnel during the war. Joan was demobilised in 1945. On her husband's return to civilian life he took up his job with the London Electricity Company, (later known as the South Eastern Electricity Board) who had been paying him a retainer of five shillings (25p) per week during the war.

I asked Joan about the availability of cosmetics in the immediate post war years; she said that she had four aunties who had remained unmarried due to the loss of potential partners in Word War One. They indulged their niece in the matter of cosmetics and other gifts. One auntie worked for Grossmith the perfumer, Joan said, "Such scents!" As far as fashion was concerned, in the immediate post-war years Joan, like most women, made do; having a sewing machine helped. Her needlework skills were put to unusual use when Bill acquired a car. It was an Austin 7 Tourer that had been up on bricks for the

Joan and Bill Henry July 1944

duration of the war. When one of its celluloid windows broke Joan would sew in a new one. She said that it was a cold car in the winter and she would take a blanket and hot water bottle on long journeys.

The couple set up home in Hawkhurst in Kent, where Bill ran the village electricity showroom. Unable to find a house to rent or buy, the couple took rooms in an old lady's house where they shared facilities. As far as food rationing was concerned, Joan said that a nearby grocer was very good at letting her know when there were any under-the-counter extras available. When she was wondering how she could add to the family income, Joan saw an advert, placed by the local butcher, offering three rooms to let in his premises, in return for housework and cooking. So she and Bill moved in and Joan, who said she could not cook very well, had to learn quickly, saying that as the boss was a butcher she knew there would be plenty of meat.

Joan and Bill were eventually able to buy a two-up-two-down cottage in Hawkhurst; it cost £500 and was much in need of repair and updating. It had only a rope banister and the lavatory was at the end of the garden. Times were hard but Bill was very good at DIY and he transformed the cottage over a period of years. Joan discovered the phenomenon of house sales and at one of these bought a length of pink carpet, cut it into strips, bound the edges and used it for the cottage stairs. Because her husband worked for SEEBOARD Joan had one of the first Hoover Twin Tub washing machines, just in time for the arrival of the couple's first child in 1950, a daughter born in a cottage hospital. Joan recalls that the matron was frequently drunk and the nurses would imprison her in her office by wedging a chair under the door. Like most villages Hawkhurst was a gossipy community and Joan said that when she went shopping, her husband would know what he was having for supper before he got home.

Joan's strongest memory of the Festival of Britain was of the samples of food, like liver *pâté*, which they brought home to eat. In all she was over-awed by everything she saw at the festival; her husband was busy picking up ideas for his DIY exploits. Joan said that he had an attic full of stuff that might come handy and was well known by the local children as being able to mend any toy. In 1954 the Hawkhurst cottage was sold for £850; the buyer went to the estate agent with the cash in her bag, as she did not trust banks. Bill and Joan bought a house for £1,800 in St Leonards where they had a son in 1957. Joan, a widow since 1983, still lives in the same road.

Marion and Arthur Henham at Hastings Registry Office October 1950

Marion and Arthur Henham

Arthur and Marion met in 1949; she was not yet sixteen when she spotted Arthur working on a building opposite to Emerson's Hardware Shop in London Road near Christ Church, where Marion was employed. Arthur, aged 24, asked if he could take Marion to the pictures and her parents agreed but said that she had to be home by 8pm. Arthur, born in Hastings Old Town, joined up in 1943; He landed in Normandy five days after the 1944 invasion began, wading ashore from "HMS Pompadour," to fight at the Battle of Hill 112 and a subsequent big battle involving the 43rd Division. Arthur eventually became part of the army of occupation in Germany; one of his duties was as an armed guard on the train that took food to Eastern Germany. He was demobilised in July 1947. In addition to the routine civilian kitting-out he was handed £51.40p, which was three months wages. He still has his army payslips, pay book and issue darning needle. Arthur recalls:

When I returned home to Hastings the sea defence blocks had been taken down and the town was starting the process of rebuilding the bombed sites. What little work was available was mainly building so for a time I had job as a bricklayer's labourer at the new Hollington School. We worked under terrific pressure; I feel as if I handled every brick in that school.

Marion and Arthur married on 21st October 1950, in Hastings Registry Office; Marion wore a burgundy hat and coat and a pale blue suit. The couple had their reception at Marion's family home and sat down to a ham salad, a luxury in those days of strict meat rationing. The newlyweds set up home with Marion's parents and stayed there for two and a half years, moving to take rooms in a house owned by Arthur's mother, in Plynlimmon Road on the West Hill. It was not a purpose-built flat and Marion found herself using a bedroom hand basin as her kitchen sink; in these awkward circumstances Marion produced the first Sunday roast dinners that are a lifelong custom in her family. Marion says:

Even though they were austerity times we never went hungry. I was also managing to pay weekly amounts at a furniture shop, saving up for when we had our own house. Our pleasures were simple; a walk along the seafront, going to the outdoor events put on for the season, like the carnival procession or the swimming galas at the Marina Bathing Pool. I made my own clothes, sewing dirndl skirts or knitting jumpers; I still do lots of knitting today.

Arthur took a job as a cleaner with the railways and by 1951 was a foreman at Slade Green, with a staff of 12. One of the tasks he supervised was the cleaning of the royal trains. In 1954, when their third child was on the way Marion and Arthur moved to a four-bedroomed council house in Bembrooke Road. Marion and Arthur have six children, three boys and three girls, 17 grandchildren and 13 great grandchildren with four more due in 2008.

When visiting Marion and Arthur I met one of their daughters, Christine a senior midwife, and her husband Martin Parsons, who, like his wife, has strong Hastings Old Town connections; the couple recently discovered that many years ago their grandmothers were Old Town neighbours and great friends. The Parsons' Royal Marine son, who was currently on leave, has served in Iraq and Afghanistan, to where he was scheduled to return in the next few months. Marion and Arthur's lounge is full of portraits of their large family, of whom they say "They have all done well in life, we are very proud of them."

Don Valentine

Don Valentine worked at St Helen's Hospital for many years, becoming its administrator for the last five years of his career and retiring in 1985. In retirement he researched and wrote the book "From Paupers to Pacemakers - The History of St Helen's Hospital." Here, he tells something of his own history:

As a teenager I was keenly interested in live entertainment in the town and regularly attended the weekly-changing plays presented at the Pier Theatre by Harry Hanson's Court Players – a very talented group of performers who lived locally. The twice yearly presentations of the Hastleons were a special delight, with often a springtime light opera production and an autumn item from their Gilbert and Sullivan repertoire. Their 1951 silver anniversary production of "Bless the Bride" was memorable – not least because it had a 26-piece orchestra in the pit of the White Rock Pavilion. I enjoyed visits to the seasons of Clarkson Rose's "Twinkle", a six weeks summer show with the programmes changing at seven day intervals. Musical entertainment, including dancing to "Eugene and his Serenaders" and the "Harmony Aces" among others, took place at the Sun Lounge, on the lower promenade, below Marine Court.

On 3rd June 1946 the Regal, one of Hastings and St Leonards seven cinemas at the time, re-opened after its wartime closure. It was a beautiful theatre; it had an organ and restaurant, as had its sister cinema, the Ritz, in Cambridge Road. The Regal was declared open by the Mayor of Hastings. The main feature film showing was "The Corn is Green," starring Bette Davis. The Ritz Cinema in Cambridge Road, later Sainsbury Supermarket and now the ESK store, was host to the Saturday morning ABC Minors Club, which was re-established when the evacuees returned home as the war reached its conclusion. My younger brother was one of the early club members: I recall him coming home, wearing his badge and whistling "Blaze Away" the tune of the club song, the last line of which ran; "We're all pals together,

Don Valentine (front. right). School clerk at St Paul's Junior and infants school. March 1946

we're minors of the ABC." The club ran for a further 25 years until the cinema's closure in 1971.

In March 1946 I left the boys' department of St Leonards Central School, Tower Road to begin work as first school clerk in nearby St Paul's Junior and Infants School, St Paul Road, where Mr William Grey was headmaster. The conditions of my employment required attendance at night school to qualify in typewriting, book-keeping grades and also shorthand, which I did not take. My memories of being employed at St Paul's School include the great respect shown by all children for their teachers. I recall Miss Dorothy Phillips reading from "The Wind in the Willows" to her Standard Class 4, for the final period of Friday afternoons, my helping to escort the children partaking of school meals to the canteen in the Mission Hall in Newgate Road. I took a portable radio to school on 20th November 1947 for the dinner ladies to hear the broadcast of the Royal Wedding ceremony. On Saturday mornings I worked in the Education Offices, 18-20 Wellington Square, most of the time under the supervision of Barry Funnell. He knew something of everything and was also part-time commander of local Sea Cadet Corp. I owe him a great debt of gratitude as he became my link to the Health Service, which eventually became my professional career.

In 1946 the terraced buildings surrounding three sides of the gardens in Wellington Square were home to a GP's surgery, the Borough Treasurer and Surveyor's Office, Public Health, Registrar, Probation services, the Baptist Church and many guest and boarding houses, as well as educational establishments. The western side of the square, on the corner of Albert Road, was graced by the Castle Hotel, which was demolished with unseemly haste by the council to make way for a branch of Tesco, which was re-located out of town within a very few years. The lower part of Wellington Square was used as the terminus for the country bus service operated by Maidstone and District Motor Services – routes to Rye, Eastbourne, Tunbridge Wells, Gillingham, Maidstone, Tenterden and Rye, via Brede. Added to their numbers were some privately-owned, single-deck buses owned by Dengates, which served the Northiam and Beckley areas. The buses, parked in regimental order on the steeply sloping incline looked ready to topple into Woolworths, which is opposite the square. At the back of

Woolworths and next to the Carlisle Hotel was a spacious bus shelter for the East Kent Road Car services which departed from the seafront for Pett, Rye, Dover, Canterbury and the Kent coastal resorts. Underneath there were public toilets and the disinfectant odour from these permeated the bus shelter. I vividly recall 23rd June 1947 when at lunch time I observed from the vantage point of the school a huge pall of black smoke to the south and seeing many people racing down Chapel Park Road. The Elite Cinema at the top of Warrior Square was a blazing inferno, on the very day it was due to re-open after a complete refurbishment following extensive war damage. I was looking forward to seeing the opening feature, "Wild Harvest." I cycled down later in the afternoon of the fire to see the ruins of the Elite.

I joined His Majesty's Service in June 1948 at RAF Padgate near Warrington to be kitted out for my two years of National Service. Afterwards I, along with others, was transferred by road and rail to The Wirral where I was to spend eight weeks of square-bashing at RAF West Kirby. I undertook trade-training (office skills) at RAF Wythall, Birmingham, followed by a nine-week posting further up north to RAF Dishforth, near Ripon. A late autumn posting to Abingdon was most welcome not least because it was within 12 miles cycling distance of two relatives. For a short time in 1949 I was a member of the station's entertainments committee, which arranged occasional dances for airmen and their families; especially remembered was when Vera Lynn was the guest star vocalist. Some of our colleagues volunteered to serve in Germany at the Berlin end of the Airlift, known as "Operation Plainfare." Abingdon being one of the RAF bases for the operation it maintained a fleet of York and Hastings aircraft carriers in its five hangers. It was a big surprise one day when the officer-in-charge of admin invited me and my close friend Maurice to take a return trip, via Malta, to the Canal Zone in Egypt on an aircraft carrying panniers for low-flying exercises over the desert. It was a great thrill to travel to Egypt with the RAF in a Hadley Page Hastings aircraft. The outward flight was trouble free: A Sunday afternoon swim in the Great Bitter Lake was most refreshing as was the Coca Cola which seemed to be on sale everywhere. During the return flight over the Sahara one of the starboard engines on our Hastings aircraft was giving trouble and on our return to Malta is was decided to have a replacement sent out from

Abingdon, so our planned overnight stay developed into a whole week at Luqa, not far from Valletta, Malta's capital. At that time the aircraft carrier was anchored in the Grand Harbour and one day we managed to see the well-known resident couple Princess Elizabeth and Prince Phillip arrive and inspect the crew on board. We saw some of the historic sights, (the buses and their drivers were indescribable) and we were able to buy confectionary as Christmas gifts for our sweet-rationed families back home in the UK. In spite of the trip having been a "dangling carrot" we decided not to sign on for further service and Maurice and I made our separate ways to demob centres in Lancashire.

After my demobilisation it was through Barry Funnell that my temporary post as a junior clerk at the newly-named St Helen's Hospital soon became permanent. In 1950, my superior was Ray McHale, the hospital's senior clerk, who loved amateur theatricals. It was not long before I became involved in some of his productions for the benefit of the patients. If not on stage I was relief accompanist or even stage manager – it provided great fun, not least for the nurses. By 1951 the hospital was beginning to grow in many ways and the administrative offices and main stores were transferred from the centre block to accommodation to the south of the hospital's main gate. During my early years at St Helens Hospital I recall being sent on Friday morning walks to the Westminster Bank in Ore to collect the wages for the weekly paid staff. With the money in a Gladstone bag and unaccompanied I walked up Church Street, which at the time was still a busy residential road. I would return the same way or via School Road and down the bank into Fredrick Road. In 1952 security stepped in and the collection of cash became the responsibility of two people in a taxi.

In 1951 Princess Elizabeth made her first visit to Hastings. I especially remember her walking along the pathway to Hastings Castle. Frank Emary was a male nurse at the hospital who was keen on 16mm cinematography and he filmed this part of the visit. He was justifiably proud when his efforts were screened to some hospital patients within three days of his filming and to the accompaniment of a 78rmp record. We ran a St Helens Hospital film season that ran from September 1950 to May 1951. A total of 63 full length programmes were presented to patients on both the hospital and residential wards. Among short films shown was the Technicolour film of the Hastings Carnival of 1950. This film was made by St Helen's male nurse Frank Emary, who had also supplied local newsreels from time to time. From these films patients were able to see the Brabazon's flight over Hastings and the opening of Darwell Reservoir. The St Helen's Hospital House Committee (Chairman Mr E A Tester) encouraged the entertainment. With extra money provided by the committee I made up banks of coloured lights, a dimming system, and gramophone turntables, to provide music from my large collection of records.

During the summer of 1951 I went on a hospital coach outing to London, first visiting the South Bank Exhibition aimed at demonstrating the British economic and technical progress since the Great Exhibition of 1851; there was much to be seen – more than could be managed in a one-day visit. I do remember some of the sights; the Skylon, the Dome of Discovery, the old Shot Tower and the resplendent Royal Festival Hall with its special modernistic feature of angled boxes in the auditorium. We saw the tree walk, fairground and the notable moving attractions created by Roland Emmet, including the Guinness Clock, concluding a memorable day at Battersea Pleasure Gardens, situated between the light-festooned Chelsea and Albert Bridges.

Irene and Derrick Burkin
(Victoria Seymour's Family)

Irene and Derrick, my brother, were married in July 1947. They met through a pen-friend scheme when Derrick was in the Royal Navy, aboard HMS Matchless and he continued his correspondence with Irene during his time in submarines. Irene says:

My borrowed wedding dress was made of white eyelet lace. I wore ordinary white sandals and had some difficulty in buying a veil and headdress due to shortages but eventually found them in London. I had the dress cleaned but didn't try it on until the day before the wedding, when I found that the side fastening would not close. The sleeves of the dress came to a point over the wrist so I cut that part off and used the fabric to make the dress fit. The eyelet fabric of the dress demanded a full-length petticoat so to save coupons I wore the dress over a parachute silk nightdress I already had. I used snippets from the nightie to edge the cut-down sleeves.

Victoria says:

Irene's three bridesmaids were two of her cousins and me. The elder of her cousins had been able to buy a new, blue crepe de chine dress; my mother used newly bought pink crepe de chine fabric to make long dresses for us two younger girls. The dress pattern was a pinafore style that could be shortened for everyday use. Austerity meant that sewing needs were practically unavailable so my mother used pieces of card to stiffen the puffed sleeves, a make-do device that did not survive the wash. My mother also crocheted the white lace gloves we wore, which were de rigueur for that period. Note the wrist bangles with a handkerchief folded over them; I think this was a fashion fad left over from the 1930s. I envied the other bridesmaids their proper sandals. Mine were just resin soles with a series of white tape loops round the edges through which cord was passed and knotted round the ankles, as in a Roman sandal. No matter how tightly the cords were tied they

Irean and Derrick Burkin, July 1947

worked loose and the wearer left the shoes behind, as I did going up the aisle. My father, a professional gardener, grew and fashioned the bridal flowers; roses for the bride and posies of sweet peas for the bridesmaids.

The wedding reception was held in a dance hall over a pub. Irene says;

Of course, my parents paid. I think the cost was six shillings and sixpence (33p) per head. This was for a sit-down two course meal and later, a tea, with cakes.. As Britain was still under austerity the food was not plentiful.

Alcohol was also in short supply; beer was the main drink but sherry was also provided; the bridegroom's parents were employed by a director of a wine import company and the sherry was a wedding gift from him. After a few bridal toasts much jollity ensued; most of the wedding guests were not accustomed to such heady drink. The newlyweds started their married life living in a room in Irene's parent's home. Irene and Derrick had two sons and four grandchildren; the first great-grandchild is expected in 2008. Derrick died in 2007, just a few weeks short of their Golden Wedding.

Hazel Comfort's mother and grandmother at the rear of the family's Church Street house

Hazel Comfort

Hazel Comfort was born in 1947 in The Croft in Hastings Old Town. Hazel's family later moved to Ore's Church Street, to its lower end where the houses overlooked the rear of the hospital buildings standing on the eastern side of Frederick Road. Hazel wishes to correct the impression of Church Street as being home to barefoot, ragged and sickly children, an idea left over from the 19th century. She said that at the lower end of the street some people owned their houses:

They had done them up to look quite nice, with the front porches painted to perfection. It was a friendly little community, with children playing happily on the plot of green, at the corner with Greville Road. None of the children were badly dressed or in want of a good meal. Their homes were cosy, everyone looked after their neighbours and doors could be left open all day long.

Each house was slightly different from the others, either two or three bedrooms, and some had steps leading to a small kitchen. Our two main bedrooms were at the top of the house – stairs went down to a small landing and a little bedroom, where my brother slept. On the floor below were the dining room and lounge and more steps led to the kitchen or scullery. None of the rooms were large. There was no bathroom and the toilet was outside, (a 1950 UK study showed that only 46% of households had a bathroom). We had a large tin bath that hung up in the corner of the scullery; the water for baths was heated in a smaller tin bath on the gas stove. When the water was hot my parents poured it into the big bath. Saturday was bath night for the children and as I was the youngest I always went first. Under the stairs was a cupboard room which was just the right size for me to play in. I kept the space as tidy as I could; with my favourite toys and a table and chair I was in my own little world, playing alone or with friends.

Some of the houses in Church Street were in a bad state; those by the spot known as the Hollow, a steep valley that led to Sandown School, were considered unsafe. As none of the houses had bathrooms and with the mental hospital so close, it was thought that everyone would be better elsewhere. Former neighbours were scattered around Hastings when the street was demolished. In 1963 we moved into a house with an indoor toilet and a bathroom and we lived there for 30 years until my mother, Hannah, died, four years after her retirement."

Hazel's mother worked for many years in the catering department of St Helen's Hospital. Hazel says:

At Christmas, a party for the staff's children was held. A large room was laid out with lots of exciting things to eat and we sat with family and friends, to feast on sandwiches, cakes, jelly and ice cream. After the food was eaten the tables were taken away and we played musical chairs, blind man's buff and had races. Then we sat on the floor, as Santa handed out the presents that our parents had donated. Each gift was wrapped, with the child's name on it. After that our parents took us home, happy, full of party food and excited about our new toys.

Ex-Inspector Charles Banks

Ex-Inspector Charles Banks, the son of a Metropolitan Police Officer, joined the Hastings force in 1932 and continued to serve the community throughout WWII. His police work was deemed a Reserved Occupation and Inspector Banks was advised by his superiors not to consider attempting to join the army as his application would be refused, even though he was a crack shot and would have made a first class sniper. His work on the Hastings Home Front was invaluable; he used his organisational abilities in setting up wartime emergency and administration offices and dealing with civilian crimes as well as the horrific aftermath of bombing raids on Hastings. In his retirement Mr Banks, now aged 94, has deployed his phenomenal memory and clear handwriting, both essential to old-time police officers, to provide contributions to this book and to various other social histories of Hastings by Victoria Seymour.

In his current contribution, Mr Banks reminds us of businesses long since gone, which in their day were the mainstay of Hastings town centre shoppers:

In Robertson Street there was Jepson's, a small but elegant department store dealing in ladies' clothing, fancy goods and stationery. After years as a scruffy indoor market it is now being refurbished as a restaurant and bar; the interior designers have retained the shop's original oak double staircase. Burton's, the gentlemen's outfitters stood at Bank Buildings, Moon's in Station Road, now demolished, famously sold tasty pork pies for six old pence each. J Sainsbury traded from a palatial shop in Wellington Place and there were four authorised news stands around the town centre's Albert Memorial. Bohemia was a flourishing shopping area, meeting most needs; Ward and Co, gentlemen's and school outfitters, had a branch there. A bye-law prohibited street singers, casual traders and stall holders from trading within 250 yards of the seafront but on Friday and Saturday barrows were allowed in Queens Road and South Terrace for the sale of fish, fruit and vegetables. In the winter Mr "Tassey" Tutt operated

Ex-Inspector Charles Banks with Jean Gill, former Senior Finance Officer at Hastings Magistrates' Courts (right) and Victoria Seaymour *a hot chestnut stall, mostly in George Street and at the Pilot Field football matches. Day trippers would arrive from London with crates of beer on the coach and already the worse for drink.*

Mr Bank's list of the former 14 hospitals and six cinemas that still existed in the post-war years brings home other changes that Hastings has undergone in the last sixty years. He continued:

The area of Hollington called Ponswood, now an industrial site, was divided into a number of smallholdings, which for some time after the war, had pig sties on them. The meat from the animals went either to butchers' shops or to family and friends. The proprietors of the piggeries used vans or horse drawn carts to collect waste from restaurants and hotels. This swill, under Animal Heath Regulations, had to be boiled for a minimum of twelve hours to obviate the risk of outbreaks of foot and mouth disease. The police checked this was properly done, in their role of Diseases of Animals Inspectors. The police carried out additional duties that have since passed to other bodies; Police Constable Les Norley was Inspector of Pleasure Boats and Police Constables Seal and Cook, police garage mechanics, were appointed Inspectors of Hackney Carriages (Taxis). The Pebsham Recreation Ground was partly used as a private flying field and Hastings Chief Constable Angus Gordon Cargill BEM, flew from Pebsham to a Scottish aerodrome to attend a police conference.

During the Hastings Week celebrations in October 2007, Ex-Inspector Charles Banks was Victoria Seymour's guest of honour at Hastings Town Hall, where she spoke about the work of the town's wartime police force. The Observer headline of the article that was published following the talk described Mr Banks as the "Real Inspector Foyle." On the 4th January 2008 he came to national attention in a Radio Times feature which took up the Observer's headline and drew comparisons and contrasts between the wartime work of the Hastings-based, fictional TV Inspector Foyle and the town's real life Inspector Banks. He is a kindly and unassuming man and is remembered with respect and affection by the police officers and civilian staff who served with and under him in the Hastings Police Force.

Biblography

From Paupers to Pacemakers ~ The History of St Helens Hospital. Don Valentine

Austerity Britain 1945-1951. David Kynaston

Old Town Walk. Old Hastings Preservation Society.

A History of Modern Britain. Andrew Marr.

The Albert Memorial. Hastings Local History Group.

The biographical manuscript on Sidney Little by Rod Osborne.

Web Sources
www.bbc.co.uk/onthisday
www.nhs/history.net
www.nationalarchives.gov.uk
www.stables-theatre.co.uk
www.metoffice.gov.uk

Letters to Hannah

written & compiled by Victoria Seymour

WWII Recollections of Hastings & South East England

Letters to Hannah looks at WWII on the Home Front through the eyes of those who lived in Hastings and South East England from September 1939 to December 1945. It also enlarges on the historical background covered in its companion book, Letters from Lavender Cottage.

Letters to Hannah visits the lives of ordinary people, who endured extraordinary times. Among many others is the account of a Battle lad, born in a cottage beside the famous 1066 battlefield. Aged fifteen he enlisted as a Home Guard, the youngest member in the country at that time, a Hastings, wartime milk delivery girl details her working and family life under fire and a young first aid volunteer highlights the horrors of bomb and machine gun attacks on civilians. 'Letters to Hannah' is rich in anecdotes and information on food rationing and shortages, the blackout, air raids, population evacuation and civil defence. The book provides a moving and factual account of wartime Hastings, the town which features in the ITV, WWII detective fiction series, Foyle's War.

Victoria Seymour links this, her second WWII social history, with a series of autobiographical letters to the future, describing her war-troubled childhood to her newborn, 21st century granddaughter, Hannah. Extracts from Letters to Hannah were included in the BBC Radio 4 history series, The Archive Hour, in July 2003.

ISBN: 0-9543901-1-3 www.victoriaseymour.com

Letters from Lavender Cottage

by Victoria Seymour

Hastings in WWII and Austerity

A collection of recently discovered letters, posted from Hastings to Canada between 1942 and 1955, inspired Victoria Seymour to compile a part-biography of their writer, Emilie Crane.

In her retirement, Emilie shared a house in Hastings, England, with her two friends, Clare and Edith and their much-loved cat, James. The almost one hundred letters Emilie sent to her Canadian cousins were initially of thanks for the food parcels they had supplied to the Lavender Cottage household in WWII and throughout the following years of harsh austerity. The letters also detail the lively and kind-hearted Emilie Crane's domestic and personal life and follow the joint fortunes of the three ageing women.

Victoria Seymour has rounded the story by adding contemporary national, local and autobiographical material. "Letters From Lavender Cottage" is a touching, human story with an informative narrative.

ISBN: 0-9543901-0-5 www.victoriaseymour.com

HOST FAMILIES WANTED

Written & compiled
by Victoria Seymour

For over half century Hastings has been host to hundreds of thousands of young people from all over the world.

Host Families Wanted, the true story of overseas English language students in Hastings, is approached with the enthusiasm for detail that Victoria Seymour's regular readers expect of her.

She recounts her own experiences as student host mother, the company director of a family-run, Hastings based language school and how the work affected her life and family.

The problem of street offences against students is considered, as are the efforts of the police and the local authority to reduce the crime and protect students.

To enrich the story there are interviews with local host families and the students' teachers. In a set of essays, a group of today's overseas students comment frankly on Hastings and their hosts.

If you are a host family, have been, or are thinking of becoming one, this book is for you.

ISBN: 0-9543901-5-6
www.victoriaseymour.com

Court in the Act

written & compiled by Victoria Seymour

Crime and Policing in WWII Hastings
Foreword by Ann Widdecombe M.P.

Victoria Seymour's Court in the Act, which completes her trilogy, concentrates on the work of the police force, the magistrates' and other courts in WWII Hastings. As the effects of war took hold, there was hardly any aspect of home front life that was not controlled by some Government Act, Regulation or Order, putting even more pressure on already overworked police officers.

There passed before the courts a parade of 'spies', aliens, pacifists, looters, wartime racketeers and small-time criminals. Added to these were thousands of usually law-abiding people who found themselves in court for flouting often not properly understood laws. Sentences were handed down that sounded like something out of 19th Century history: A fine for stealing one onion from an allotment, a few apples from a tree or vegetable peelings from a dustbin or a month in prison for allowing light to escape from behind a curtain.

Meanwhile, the formidable Government Enforcers stalked the land incognito, seeking to trap unwary traders and citizens and bring them to justice. Police Court reports from the period 1939 to 1945 give an insight into a little discussed aspect of WWII. 'Vigilant', The Hastings and St Leonards Observer 1940s columnist, provides a background, with comment on the foibles and morals of a seaside town under fire.

Fact met fiction, when in 2004 Victoria Seymour was asked by Greenlit Productions, who film Foyle's War, the WWII detective television drama set in Hastings, to assist in re-creating a Hastings' wartime magistrates' court for series three.